Marine Life
of the Caribbean

Alick Jones and Nancy Sefton

MACMILLAN
CARIBBEAN

Macmillan Education
Between Towns Road, Oxford OX4 3PP
A division of Macmillan Publishers Limited
Companies and representatives throughout the world

www.macmillan-caribbean.com

ISBN 0 333 93048 7

First published 2002

Typeset by CjB Editorial Plus
Illustrated by TechType
Cover design by Gary Fielder, AC Design
Cover photographs by Nancy Sefton

Printed and bound in Malaysia

2006 2005 2004 2003 2002
10 9 8 7 6 5 4 3 2 1

Contents

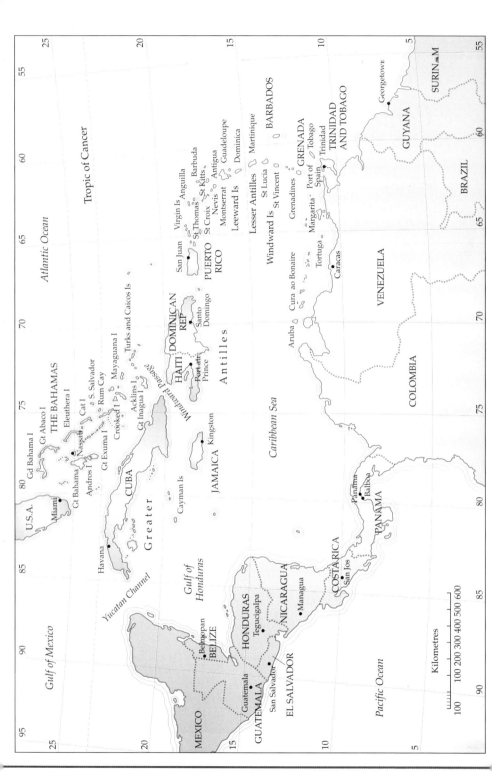

Preface

This is the third stage of development of this book. In 1975 the first version by Nancy Sefton alone and entitled *Guide to the Marine Life of the Cayman Islands* was published by the Cayman Islands Conservation Association. Alick Jones was approached by the Caribbean Conservation Association with a view to upgrading this version to cover all of the Caribbean. That project resulted in the first edition of *Marine Life of the Caribbean* being published by Macmillan Education in 1978. After more than 20 years in print, it seemed as though a new edition was overdue. This edition has a revised and enlarged text together with all-colour illustrations replacing the dominantly black and white photographs of the 1978 edition.

During the preparation of this edition Alick Jones would like to acknowledge help from a variety of people and organizations. In Jamaica, George and Monica Warner were hospitable and supportive including making use of office space and access to documents and data at the Center for Marine Sciences, UWI (Mona). He was also able to make use of the University's marine stations at Discovery Bay and Port Royal. Staff at both stations were helpful but Marlon Hibbert deserves a special vote of thanks for organizing trips into the Port Royal mangrove swamps. A number of the academic staff of UWI also gave of their time, especially Mona Webber and Karl Aitken – the latter also made his huge slide collection relating to Caribbean fisheries available for inspection. We have used a number of his images. As always in these endeavours, spouses find themselves fulfilling a number of unaccustomed and unexpected roles. In Sarah Jones's case, finding that which was lost (cameras, books, spectacles, computer disks, mask and fins, etc.) was only one of a myriad (mostly more intellectual) ways in which she contributed.

Acknowledgements

The authors and publishers wish to acknowledge, with thanks, the following photographic sources:

Karl Aiken: Figs 7.6, 7.8, 9.7, 9.8

Corbis: Fig 7.1

Scott A. Eckert: Figs 8.2, 8.3, 8.4, 8.6, 8.7, 8.8, 8.9

Alick Jones: Figs 1.2, 1.3, 1.4, 1.7, 2.2, 2.3, 2.5, 2.6, 2.7, 2.10, 2.11, 2.12, 2.13, 2.16, 2.17, 3.4, 3.5, 3.7, 3.8, 3.9, 3.10, 4.1, 4.2, 4.3, 4.4, 4.5, 4.6, 4.7, 4.8, 5.1, 5.2, 5.3, 5.4, 5.5, 5.6, 5.7, 5.8a, b, 5.9, 6.1, 6.2, 6.6, 6.7, 6.12, 6.13, 6.14, 6.15, 6.36, 6.58, 7.3, 7.4, 7.5, 7.7, 8.10, 8.11, 8.12, 9.1, 9.2, 9.4, 9.5, 9.6, 9.9, 9.10, 9.11, 9.12, 9.14, 9.15, 9.16

Science Photo Library: Figs 1.5 (Stephen and Donna O'Meara), 1.6 (NASA/Goddard Space Flight Centre), 7.9 (Gregory Ochocki), 8.13 (Douglas Faulkner), 8.14 (Ron Sandford), 8.15 (Lawrence Naylor)

Nancy Sefton: Figs 1.1, 2.1, 2.4, 2.14, 3.1, 3.2, 3.3, 3.6, 6.3, 6.4, 6.5, 6.8, 6.9, 6.10, 6.11, 6.18, 6.19, 6.20, 6.21, 6.22, 6.23, 6.24, 6.25, 6.26, 6.27, 6.28, 6.29, 6.30, 6.31, 6.32, 6.33, 6.34. 6.35, 6.37, 6.38, 6.39, 6.40, 6.41, 6.42, 6.44, 6.45, 6.46, 6.47, 6.48, 6.49, 6.50, 6.51, 6.52, 6.53, 6.54, 6.55, 6.56, 6.57, 6.59, 6.60, 6.61, 6.62, 6.63, 6.64, 8.1, 8.5, 9.3, 9.13

Southampton Oceanography Centre: Fig 7.2

Ian F. Took: Fig 6.43

George Warner: Figs 6.16, 6.17

The publishers have made every effort to trace the copyright holders, but if they have inadvertently overlooked any, they will be pleased to make the necessary arrangements at the first opportunity.

1 The Region

INTRODUCTION

The Caribbean! The very name conjures up a vision of sunshine, warmth and, above all, sparkling sea and golden sand. The image is often one of idyllic beauty and a pristine unspoiled purity, almost a present-day Garden of Eden. Indeed there is much to support this view of the region, not least in the wonderful variety of animals and plants that inhabit the sea and its fringes. These creatures are grouped together into assemblages of astonishing complexity often interdependent one with the other. However, as with any other part of the world, there are some aspects of the natural world which give cause for concern. Some, but not all, of these situations may

Fig 1.1 This must be close to most people's vision of a Caribbean beach. We need to work hard to preserve this paradise.

1

Fig 1.2 All of the major marine habitats of the Caribbean can be seen in this photograph. In the right foreground is a red mangrove tree emerging from the sea (unusually on a rocky outcrop). In the shallower water paler sandy areas and darker seagrass beds can be seen. Beyond, in the distance, the surf can be glimpsed as it breaks on the fringing coral reef. Beyond that again is the open sea.

be caused by man's presence and in most there is something that can be done to alleviate the problem. Knowledge and understanding are the key although no amount of these can be effective without the will and ability to act. This book attempts to offer the reader an introduction to the beauty and fascination of the marine creatures of the Caribbean and the habitats in which they live. It is hoped that the account will generate interest and enthusiasm in the reader for this wonderful watery world. For those new to the region, perhaps it will bring a spark of desire to help conserve and preserve its treasures for future generations. For those already committed, perhaps the book will further enlighten and inspire.

We have arranged this book so that each of the major ecosystems (mangrove swamps, seagrass beds, coral reefs and so on) is dealt with in turn. The book is not intended as simply an identification guide; rather it tries to explain the nature of the contribution that the animals and plants make to their community.

The Caribbean Sea is usually regarded as that portion of the ocean bordered to the east by the island chain of the Lesser Antilles, to the north by the Greater Antilles and to the west and south by the mainland of Central and South America. There are other near-by areas with considerable similarities in terms of their marine ecosystems. In particular the vast area of shallow Atlantic forming the Bahamas Bank with its low emergent islands contains some of the best examples of corals reefs and related habitats in the region. Parts of Florida together with the northern island of Bermuda show features in common with what is regarded as 'typically' Caribbean. Thus for the purposes of this book much of what is written applies to this wider concept of the Caribbean. The Gulf of Mexico lies to the north and communicates with the Caribbean in particular through the Yucatan Channel between Mexico and Cuba. However, its characteristics are somewhat different from the Caribbean in that it does not have the same easy communication with the open Atlantic and is much affected by the influx of fresh water and sed-iment from many major river systems including the Mississippi. To the south the great river systems of continental south America so affect the marine environment that many of the animals and plants typical of the Caribbean are absent. The area under consideration lies roughly between 27°N and 8°N and constitutes an area of about 1.1 million square miles (2.7 million square kilometres).

Most individuals have a particular and personal view of the Caribbean coastline. Most visitors will have had experience of rela-tively few places in the region, typically a few islands. For the local inhabitants clearly their home environment will dominate their vision of 'The Caribbean'. For visitors the vision is usually one of islands and golden beaches with coral reefs to dive on and snorkel over, but we should not forget the thousands of miles of mainland coastline in many cases dominated by rocky coasts or fringed with mangroves. Nor must we forget the extremely varied and complex cultural and linguistic heritage that affects the attitude and percep-tion of visitors and locals alike. In respect of the marine environ-ments, relative development and wealth along with the ways in which the sea is exploited will be of importance in forging policies and actions. In light of this extreme diversity in the physical, bio-logical, cultural and financial backgrounds to the marine environ-ment of the region, is there any hope of being able to make valid generalizations about Caribbean marine biology? The answer is a resounding 'yes'. The major ecosystems function in similar ways and face very similar threats and hazards throughout the region.

A major problem faced by the countries with Caribbean coast-line is that of preserving their natural features in the face of the

Fig 1.3 Coastal development frequently threatens inshore environments. Although one tends to think in terms of large hotel blocks and apartments there is much demand for smaller housing projects. Even these pose problems and are sometimes less easily controlled.

threat to them posed by the demand for improved living standards: the building of more houses; the cutting down of trees; the making of roads; the establishment of factories; and the need to dispose of their waste products into the air and sea. The encouragement of tourism is a considerable contributor to this list of destructive items through additional building and, in many cases, damage to the beaches, reefs and swamps. However, the realization that tourists value the marine environment can also be a positive factor favouring greater efforts to preserve and conserve the natural heritage.

It is the beaches, reefs and swamps, with all that they contain, that are the subject of this book. The Caribbean marine environment is one of immense richness: the mangroves with their birds, insects and fish; the reefs with their corals of every imaginable size, shape and colour, and their abundance of other animals and plants; and the deeper seas beyond the reefs with their characteristic fish.

It is an environment that is not only full of interest for the beholder but also of significance for the ecology and the economy of the whole region. Damage to any part of it whether by predatory visitors, sewage from hotels, effluents from factories, or oil

Fig 1.4 Oil from leaking ships or from tanker flushing often results in small spills that can wash up on to the shore. This creates unsightly deposits which are a nuisance to beach users as well as being a toxic hazard for flora and fauna. This thick clot of oil on a rocky shore will persist for weeks.

discharged from tankers, sets up a chain reaction with far reaching effects not only on the fisheries and other aspects of the marine environment but also on the shape of the beaches, the nature of the land and the availability of food supplies. In time, very serious changes could take place that would not only destroy the natural beauty of these islands but also undermine the economic structure, particularly that part of it resulting from tourism.

THE LAND

Nine countries of continental America border the Caribbean. A considerable portion of this coastline is fringed with mangrove swamps thriving on the sediment washed down by the rivers and lining the sheltered bays and estuaries. There are also many long sandy beaches sometimes with fine coral reefs offshore; those in Belize are particularly famous for their beauty.

The islands of the Caribbean vary in size from Cuba (44,218 square miles (114,524 square kilometres); larger than the state of Kentucky and twice the size of Ireland) down to the tiny uninhabited islets of the northeastern part of the sea. They vary in geological origin and it is this that produces the great variety of coastal scenery. The large islands of the Greater Antilles – Cuba, Hispaniola, Jamaica and Puerto Rico – have a volcanic origin but active volcanism has ceased long ago. Sedimentary and coral rocks have been added to their igneous core and their long history has meant that there has been time for the rocks to be lifted, folded and eroded. As a result these islands have a complicated structure and many types of scenery.

The islands of the Lesser Antilles, stretching from the Virgin Islands in the north to Grenada in the south, are also of largely volcanic origin but they are much more recent with the youngest islands at the southern end of the chain. Volcanic activity is still widespread. In 1902, Mt Pelee in Martinique erupted violently and it is said that all but one of the 40,000 inhabitants of St Pierre perished. (The survivor was a condemned criminal awaiting execution in a tiny ill-ventilated cell that kept out the rush of superheated

Fig 1.5 An aerial view of the eruption of the Soufriere Hills volcano, Montserrat. Gases and ash rise from the volcano while solid material has moved by pyroclastic flow down the hillside to the sea where a delta of sediment has formed. This photograph was taken on 2nd April 1997.

vapour resulting from the explosive eruption; he was subsequently granted a pardon thus escaping death twice over!) In the same year La Soufrière in St Vincent erupted killing 2000 people. La Soufrière in Guadeloupe underwent violent activity in 1976 but there was no major eruption. More recently we have seen the beautiful island of Montserrat devastated and all but rendered uninhabitable by a series of eruptions which started on 18 July 1995 and which are still continuing at the time of writing (February 2001). A major event in June 1997 resulted in the extrusion of large amounts of ash and hot gases (pyroclastic flow) which inundated or destroyed numerous habitations and resulted in the tragic loss of 19 lives. Six months later there was a major collapse of the old volcanic edifice at which time it was estimated that blast was escaping from the crater at a speed of over 300 ft (100 m) per second and that ash was being blown out at a rate of over 40,000 cubic yards (30,000 m^3) per second. The main problem has been one of ash covering land and buildings alike, driving out the population from all but the northern end of the island and of course future activity is uncertain. Similar eruptions cannot be ruled out on other islands with active volcanoes.

Hot springs abound on many of the islands and volcanically produced steam has a potential for generating electricity on at least two islands. The volcanic islands frequently have black beaches, the grains being composed of tiny larval rock fragments. Barbados is very much the exception to this general picture of the smaller islands. It is a flat coral cap sitting on a core of much older sedimentary rock. Antigua is not wholly volcanic either but has fairly recent limestone and other sedimentary rocks as well as igneous ones. Trinidad, the most southerly of the islands, has only recently separated from Venezuela and like her possesses oil and gas fields of great commercial value.

In one area of the Caribbean the islands lie in very shallow water. These are the Bahamas, made of continental rock to the north but rock of volcanic origin to the south. They are surrounded by tens of thousands of square miles of water only 33 feet (10 m) or so deep. This shallow sea is a classic site of active limestone formation. The water is saturated with calcium carbonate and as the sun heats it up evaporation takes place resulting in the precipitation of the limestone. This process is thought to have been going on for 130 million years and the limestone created may be as much as 10,000 feet (3300 m) thick. As it is formed the whole mass sinks into the earth's crust because of its enormous weight.

THE SEA

The position of the Caribbean, which lies mostly south of the Tropic of Cancer, results in sea temperatures which are high and fairly constant; for instance in Barbados they vary during the year between 25.5 and 27.7°C. Further north the sea is cooler and shows greater seasonal variation, but even in Florida the mean annual temperature is higher than 25°C and never falls below 20°C. This is particularly important as coral reef formation does not occur below the latter temperature. The salinity is also high and stable. Only at the mouths of large rivers (e.g. Orinoco) does fresh water affect the marine fauna to any extent. 'Bubbles' of water of reduced salinity from the mouth of the Amazon do travel northwards into the region, but by the time they arrive their influence is negligible.

The major current movements in the Caribbean are an extension of the South Equatorial Current. This sweeps across the breadth of the Atlantic from the west coast of Africa, and along the northeast coast of South America. It passes into the Caribbean running in a roughly westerly direction (drift bottles released in Barbados have been recovered from Nicaragua). The current then turns to the north to pass into the Gulf of Mexico through the Yukatan Channel. This water finally passes out into the Atlantic again to form the Gulf Stream. Some surface water also enters the Caribbean from the North Equatorial Current passing both north and south of the Greater Antilles.

Much of the water moving in the South Equatorial Current has welled up from the deep ocean along the southwest coast of Africa in the Benguela Current. This cold uprising water is very rich in nutrients and the ocean in that region is very productive. However, by the time the water has moved across the Atlantic, the floating animals and plants have removed most of these nutrients. Many of these creatures are eaten or die and sink to the ocean floor. This means that the Caribbean waters are poor in nutrients, unproductive and contain relatively few living organisms: a situation typical of most tropical oceans and seas. Thus the fisheries of the region, although important and probably capable of some further exploitation, will never be as rich as those in many temperate regions or areas of upwelling.

Although the productivity of the open Caribbean is low this is not the case for some of the coastal areas. Both mangrove swamps and coral reefs are capable of producing anything up to 40 times as much living material per unit area as the barren sea. In the mangrove swamps the sparse nutrients of the sea are supplemented by drainage from the land as well as by large quantities of rotting leaves and so on from the trees and other plants. In coral reefs the high productivity is partly due to the way in which the nutrients are passed from one member of the community to another in an efficient way, so that they are prevented from leaving the reef to enter the open sea. The remarkable symbiosis between the coral organisms and their zooxanthellae (see page 58) is also responsible for the striking difference between the richness of the reef and the poverty of the open sea.

Most of the Caribbean Sea is deep (the average depth is about 7220 feet (2200 m) so there is little area of continental shelf. This contrasts with the area around the large landmasses which often have a fringing area many miles wide which is relatively shallow, averaging about 250 feet (76 m). Only in a few places are there large areas of the Caribbean which are so shallow (south of Cuba, the Bahamas Bank and between Jamaica and Nicaragua), elsewhere the land falls steeply into the sea. In one or two places the depths are great by any standards, for example the Cayman Trench just south of the Cayman Islands is over 22,000 feet (7000 m) deep. Steep shorelines combined with small tides, often only 8 inches (20 cm) or so, mean that the intertidal zone (that which is exposed to the air at low tide) is relatively narrow. This is another point of contrast between the Caribbean and many non-tropical areas.

THE WEATHER

The weather in the Caribbean is usually stable, especially as it affects marine environments, and because of its position close to the equator seasonal influences are usually slight. The only feature of the weather to have a profound effect on the marine environment is the hurricane. These violent cyclonic storms are usually spawned over equatorial oceans, in our case the Atlantic. Summer heating of the Saharan Desert results in temperature inversion as compared with the west coast of Africa. This in turn results in socalled 'easterly waves' which move out over the ocean. Where high sea surface temperatures exist (at least 26.5°C) spirals of moist warm air develop. Guided by the Trade Winds they move in a westerly direction towards the Caribbean where they often veer towards

Fig 1.6 A satellite image of a hurricane moving towards Florida having already passed over the Bahamas. This hurricane (named 'Floyd') caused 40 deaths in Florida and contained winds which reached 140 mph (225 kmph).

the north. Thus on the whole the more southerly islands suffer the least. A hurricane is defined as a tropical storm with winds of over 74 mph (118 kmph) although gusts may frequently exceed this value. Hurricanes are classified according to their severity by the Saffir–Simpson scale: category 1 has winds of 74–95 mph (118–152 kmph); category 2 has winds of 96–110 mph (154–176 kmph) and so on up to the most severe category 5 with winds in excess of 155 mph (248 kmph). These latter are fortunately rare with only two crossing coastlines in the 70 years between 1925 and 1995 whereas in the same period there were 124 rated category 3 or lower. There are about ten tropical storms each year in or near the region and of these about six will develop into hurricanes. Many of these will travel only over deep ocean doing little damage. About two each year are expected to pass over shallow sea and coastlines. In the Caribbean the hurricane season is from June until November peaking between mid-August and October.

There is evidence accumulating that Caribbean hurricanes are influenced not only by Atlantic weather systems. Complex weather and ocean current interactions occur in the Pacific, in particular the so-called El Niño and La Niña effects. In years when the former has prevailed it has been blamed for dramatic weather changes all around the Pacific Basin. However, those years seem also to produce fewer hurricanes in our region. In years when La Niña is the dominant influence Caribbean hurricanes are more frequent; a fine example of the proverb 'It is an ill wind that blows nobody good'.

Damage to marine environments results from a number of features of these hurricanes. The strong winds not only provoke large and destructive waves but also build up a storm surge in front of the cyclonic system. When this meets a coastline it may be 10 feet (3 m) high and 50–100 miles wide. If this surge coincides with a high tide the effect may be even more profound. Such activity will clearly result in widespread inundation and flooding of near-shore areas wreaking havoc in mangrove swamps, over beaches and seagrass beds as well as battering rocky shores and coral reefs. Such infrequent but catastrophic events may well be long-term limiting factors in the establishment of viable reefs in what seem to be otherwise suitable sites. Hurricane Hattie, which swept over part of the Belize coast in 1961, destroyed about 90 per cent of the corals in some places and it has been established that recovery *at favourable sites* could take 25–30 years and much longer in other places. Mangrove vegetation will also suffer if the winds are strong enough to break branches or fell whole trees (which they often are). The potential damage due to wind increases exponentially with wind velocity. Thus the effects of 148 mph (237 kmph) would be expected to be 250 times that of a velocity of 74 mph (118 kmph).

Heavy rain can also cause heavy mortality of marine animals living in shallow water. In Kingston harbour, Jamaica, for example, almost complete destruction of attached marine animals was reported following rainstorms during which over 4 inches (10 cm) of rain fell in 24 hours. The harbour is, however, a very confined water mass and on open coasts rainwater usually has little effect. However, considering that the average hurricane generates wind energy equalling about half the worldwide electrical generating capacity, perhaps we should consider ourselves lucky that the effects are not worse.

THE TIDES

Moon generated tides are usually small in the Caribbean. Typical values range from about 6 inches (15 cm) for Jamaica and Columbia, 8 inches (20 cm) for Belize to 24 inches (60 cm) for

Bahamas. There are some exceptions including Costa Rica (Punta Arenas) with 8.5 feet (260 cm). However, it is not uncommon to hear the term 'tides' used (incorrectly) to describe ocean currents. The small lunar tides mean that there is only a small area of the inshore environment which is uncovered and covered twice daily. Indeed the wave and surf action often almost obliterates the tidal variation. On rocky shores this often results in wave action being concentrated at one particular level on vertical surfaces. This results in erosion and an undercut profile typical of so many Caribbean rock beaches. In mangrove swamps, however, where waves are usually absent, the tides have a real influence and many of the animals are adapted to cope with periods of both immersion and emersion.

Fig 1.7 Tides in the Caribbean are relatively small compared to many other parts of the world. This picture, taken at about mid-tide, shows the maximum high tide mark as a yellowish bar about half way up the ruler

2 The Middle World
of the Mangroves

Nearly 25 per cent of the coastline of the Caribbean Sea is occupied by a rich natural community called the mangrove. It is dominated by trees of *Rhizophora mangle*, the red mangrove, and reaches its best development in estuaries, on sheltered coasts near the mouths of large rivers which bring down silt and on bordering coastal lagoons. Such conditions are found along the south coasts of Cuba, Puerto Rico and Jamaica, where the mangroves grow also on coral reefs, in the North Sound on Grand Cayman, the Gulf of Paria coast of Trinidad, areas of Central America such as Yucatan and Panama and northern South America in localities like the Cienaga Grande of Colombia. Small patches of mangrove vegetation occur on almost all the West Indian islands, but only in estuarine or lagoonal situations do mangrove swamps develop.

THE TREES

Rhizophora has a branching prop-root system which supports it on soft muds in the intertidal region. Once established, the trees encroach on the sea by further prop-root extension and have been described as 'walking out to sea'. The tangled mass of roots traps debris and silt and thus encourages sedimentation, so that the swamp is extended gradually seawards. This is further aided by the seedlings which grow on the seaward side of the *Rhizophora* as they fall from the parent tree. Unlike most familiar trees, the seed grows while the fruit is still attached to the branches. Soon a slender seedling emerges from the end of the fruit growing ever downwards. By the time it drops it is from 7 to 14 inches (18 to 36 cm) long, and dart-shaped. When it falls it penetrates some distance into the mud where it becomes established. The seedling grows rapidly, its height increasing to 24 inches (60 cm) in the first year.

Fig 2.1 Mangroves act as a buffer between land and sea. They can also gradually grow out in a seawards direction, thus reclaiming land.

In its second year, it begins to send out prop-roots for support. So, a new mangrove area is born, or an old one expanded. The red mangroves are 'pioneer' plants on coastal mudflats, but once the sediments are stabilized and their level raised to near high tide level, seeds of the black mangrove, *Avicennia germinans*, can germinate successfully. Lacking prop-roots, the black mangroves send small, woody fingers up through the ground. These pneumatophores enable the trees to obtain directly from the air the oxygen which is lacking in the peaty sediments. This dense root network produced by the black mangroves helps to consolidate further the swamp sediments, eventually rendering them suitable for colonization by the buttonwood, *Conocarpus erectus*, and other land plants. In this way, three zones of mangrove vegetation are produced. The red mangroves with their distinctive prop-roots are submerged in salt water at high tide. Inland from these are the black mangroves, occupying the upper tidal zone in a swampy environment, and then come the buttonwoods, which are typical of the landward fringes of swamps. In some islands a zone of the white mangrove, *Laguncularia racemosa*, occurs between the black and button mangroves. This is especially true where dry or sandy soils

Fig 2.2 Flowers of the red mangrove, *Rhizophora mangle*.

Fig 2.3 Young fruits of the red mangrove.

Fig 2.4 The mature fruit of the red mangrove. The seedling root is already developed. If it falls from the tree into mud it will pierce the substrate and remain upright as it continues to grow (see Fig 2.5). If it falls into water it will float until it is washed ashore when it will grow if conditions are favourable.

Fig 2.5 This recently dropped red mangrove fruit is well established and has produced its first leaves.

Fig 2.6 The black mangrove, *Avicennia germinans* lives in somewhat drier conditions than red mangrove, usually the soil is anaerobic mud. For the roots to gain oxygen the plant has special air-breathing roots (pneumatophores) seen in this photograph.

occur, but *Laguncularia* is found more commonly as scattered individuals among the zones of red and black species.

Although mangroves seem to have an 'easy' life this is not really the case. For instance, although they grow in waterlogged or damp conditions the salt in the water makes it difficult for the mangroves to take water in through their roots. Thus they are in danger of losing more water by evaporation (transpiration as it is called in plants) from the leaves than can be replaced through the roots. As a result they exhibit a number of features which are more usually found in plants from dry conditions, in particular thick leaves with heavy waxy cuticles. It is this cuticle which gives the leaves their characteristic sheen. It is also significant that mangroves do well in conditions of high humidity and cloudiness, factors which reduce transpiration. Interestingly, these same factors seem to be of importance in the development of tropical rain forests. The waterlogged soils also make it difficult for the roots to 'breathe' and as a result the black mangroves, as has been mentioned earlier, possess pneumatophores which grow up into the air. It is a characteristic of demanding or difficult habitats that the range of successful species is restricted and again this is borne out by the handful of tree species found in these swamps. However, although it may be a difficult habitat for the trees it certainly is not so for the animals that thrive there.

Fig 2.7 Although mangroves grow in damp or waterlogged sites they have difficulty in gaining water because of the sea salt.

THE MANGROVE COMMUNITY

On close study a variety of living things is found in the mangrove areas. This community of interdependent organisms makes mangrove areas among the most productive in tropical regions. Nesting and roosting in the upper limbs of the mangrove trees are tropical birds such as pelicans, frigate birds, cattle egrets and the little blue heron. Nearby, spiders spin webs among the leaves to catch the sandflies and mosquitoes that breed in pools of dark water below. Other insects such as wasps and dragonflies dart busily above the damp roots. Ever watchful for a meal of insects are the anolis lizards, iguanas and geckos, slithering about the branches. Tree snails, *Littorina*, crawl along the tree trunks, leaving behind their silver trails. Certain species of crabs, rarely found in any other environment, inhabit this tangled world of roots and branches. They are predatory crabs like *Goniopsis*, *Pachygrapsus* and *Sesarma*, and the tree crab *Aratus*, which feeds on leaves, bark and algae.

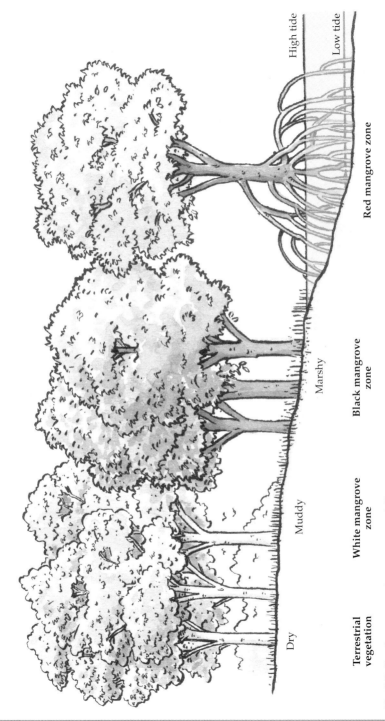

Fig 2.8 The three zones of mangrove vegetation.

Terrestrial vegetation

White mangrove zone

Black mangrove zone

Red mangrove zone

Dry

Muddy

Marshy

High tide

Low tide

Fig 2.9 The mangrove community.

Fig 2.10 The mangrove crab, *Aratus pisonii*, is a common inhabitant of the swamps, scrambling among the branches well above water level.

Fig 2.11 Below water level the prop-roots of red mangrove are covered with attached plants and animals. Tube worms and a blue-lipped oyster are easily visible here.

At the water line clusters of oysters cling to the red mangrove roots. There are two common species: the mangrove oyster, *Crassostrea*, most often found in brackish water regions; and the flat tree oyster, *Isognomon*, of more saline habitats. Attached to the roots, their shells are parted so they can draw in the nutrient-rich water which they strain for food particles. If properly prepared for the table, oysters of both types are very tasty, so these shellfish are much sought after for food. Fishes with strong teeth, like puffers, also find them a perfect meal and *Murex* snails drill through the shells to get at the meat. Starfish are capable of prising the shells apart and inserting their stomach to digest the oyster flesh. Some birds also feast on the mangrove oysters, by poking their sharp bills in-between the shells and severing the muscle that holds them closed.

By far the most colourful growth on the roots is that of the sponges. Orange, red, blue and yellow encrusting species compete for space here. These draw water in through microscopic pores, filter out the food particles, and eject the water through larger holes

Fig 2.12 Pink sponges dominate this piece of mangrove root.

Fig 2.13 Colonies of sea-squirts (ascidians) are common on mangrove roots.

which are visible to the naked eye. The sponges grow largely below the water line of low tide, where many other types of marine animal occur. Colonies of transparent tunicates cling to the roots in this zone. Tunicates, whose popular name is 'sea-squirts', are mostly small animals looking like elongated bubbles. They siphon water through the body, feeding on the microscopic food particles it contains. Although these creatures are found on the open reefs as well, they exist in greatest abundance in the mangrove. Small sea anemones attach themselves to the roots, their long tentacles spreading to capture food organisms which are then transferred to a central mouth. Larger anemones may be seen attached to the sides of lagoons just below the tangled root network; the large solitary species *Condylactis gigantia*, found here frequently, is also a common reef dweller. Back among the roots, well hidden from view, juvenile fish of many species live until they are mature enough to migrate to the open sea or to neighbouring reefs. Young butterflyfish, angelfish, tarpon, snappers and barracudas peer out from the tangled roots, which are a perfect refuge. Sharing this nursery are juvenile spiny lobsters and shrimps, also destined to take up life in the open sea when they are older.

Resting in and on the mud below the mangroves are worms, small crustaceans and fat sea cucumbers. Perhaps the most bizarre marine resident of mangroves is the large jellyfish *Cassiopeia*, which can be seen resting on the bottom of lagoons and water channels.

Fig 2.14 Mangrove swamps are nursery grounds for many animals that live out their adult lives in deeper water. Here a group of juvenile snappers lurk in the mangrove roots.

In the Caribbean region there are two species of these jellyfish: *Cassiopeia frondosa* and *Cassiopeia xamachana*. They lie upside down on the muddy bottom, pulsating; their complex branched tentacles spread upward to capture food particles floating in the tea-coloured waters. These jellyfish have a life span of 18 months and the largest specimens reach a diameter of 12 inches (30 cm). They are normally absent from estuarine mangrove areas where salinities are probably too low. Along the side of inlets and channels, short-spined sea urchins of the species *Lytechinus variegatus* cling to roots and fallen leaves, feeding on the abundant algae. Sea urchins are grazers, both here and on the open reefs, being especially common in beds of the seagrass *Thalassia*, which may grow among the mangrove roots. A delicate and beautiful creature is the shell-less snail called a nudibranch or sea slug. Nudibranchs are seen infrequently on coral reefs and rocky shores, but are abundant among the roots in mangrove swamps. The most common genus, *Elysta*, is coloured pale green and blends perfectly with its background of fallen leaves and marine grasses.

On the drier parts of the swamp, away from the water's edge where the ground is covered with the black mangroves' pneumatophores, there often live teeming hundreds of fiddler crabs (*Uca* spp.). These charming little crabs live in burrows of often 0.75 to 1.2 inches (2 or 3 cm) in diameter. The name derives from the male of the species which has one claw much enlarged, and often brightly coloured. In display behaviour, this claw is waved across the crab's 'face' almost in the manner of a violin bow and it is this that gives rise to the name of 'fiddler'. The display claw is so large it cannot be used for feeding and is simply a status symbol to frighten other males and to attract females (there is some doubt about its efficiency here!). Occasionally males will indulge in fights but more usually the matter is settled by a bout of claw waving. The females, with typical good sense, retain two small but useful claws which are both used for feeding. The food is often tiny pieces of detritus picked from semi-solid mud surfaces uncovered when the tide is out.

THE MANGROVE FOOD WEB

The productive nature of a swamp is based on a pattern of interdependence among its great variety of life forms. This feeding pattern, based on who eats whom, is a balanced system that sustains

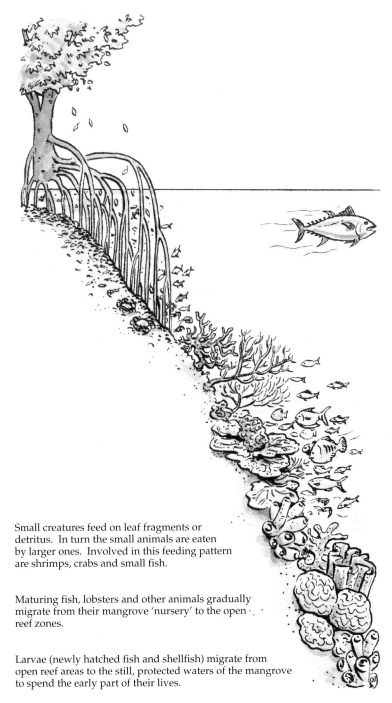

Small creatures feed on leaf fragments or detritus. In turn the small animals are eaten by larger ones. Involved in this feeding pattern are shrimps, crabs and small fish.

Maturing fish, lobsters and other animals gradually migrate from their mangrove 'nursery' to the open reef zones.

Larvae (newly hatched fish and shellfish) migrate from open reef areas to the still, protected waters of the mangrove to spend the early part of their lives.

Fig 2.15 Food web.

life here in the mangrove and affects the offshore reefs and other habitats, and is termed a 'food web'. This intricate food web starts with the mangrove leaves. Their lives spent, they fall to the mud below or into the water where they become coated with bacteria and fungi. Gradually over the months the leaves are broken down by these decomposer organisms into smaller and smaller pieces. These fragments of organic matter are now referred to as detritus.

Attracted to this rich banquet are shellfish, shrimps, crabs, worms, insect larvae and fish. In some mangrove areas, leaf detritus accounts for up to 90 per cent of the diet of such animals. These detritus feeders in turn become the prey of several dozen species of juvenile fish and of larger invertebrates. Much of the particulate matter produced from the breakdown of mangrove leaves, fruit, flowers and twigs is transported out of the mangrove areas and forms the base of other food webs in other habitats. Those who view mangrove areas as wasteland to be filled with dredged material for conversion to building lots or agricultural land are blind to the role that mangroves play in the interdependence of tropical marine ecosystems and their productivity.

Fig 2.16 The floor of the drier parts of mangrove swamps is covered with leaf-litter which is a rich source of energy and nutrients at the base of the mangrove food web. Indeed most mangrove swamps export these essentials into the open sea.

Fig 2.17 Mature red mangroves with their gothic tracery of prop-roots.

THE IMPORTANCE OF THE MANGROVE

As hinted in the previous paragraphs, mangrove areas are important to Man in several ways. It has already been explained that mangroves are land builders. As the colony of red and black mangroves increases, broken limbs, leaves and sediment accumulate and decay of roots in the soil leads to the formation of peat. Shells of shellfish, crabs and other animals are deposited also, and in some areas coral rubble is trapped among the prop-roots, building the shoreline up to a level where coconut palms, sea grape or other littoral plants may take root. In this way the land is extended slowly to seaward.

Mangroves grow most commonly on sheltered shores but in stormy weather the trees along the coastline become a vital buffer zone, protecting the land behind from erosion by high waves and hurricane flooding. It is likely also that mangroves filter off some of the land-derived pollutants, thus protecting coral reefs and other littoral habitats from damage.

Perhaps the most important role of the mangroves is the production of a rich variety of food organisms. Many of these, such as fish, oysters, mussels, conch, crabs and birds, can be harvested in the swamps and the production of protein from these sources is higher than from equivalent areas of agricultural land. The swamps provide food and shelter for a variety of creatures, including juvenile fish and crustaceans, destined to populate coastal and offshore areas where they will be harvested eventually during fishing operations.

It is obvious that we must learn to place a much higher value on this mangrove ecosystem which plays such an important part in the natural balance of life on and around the Caribbean islands.

3 Life in Sand

The Caribbean is rightly famous among tourists for its beaches, be they golden, white or black. It is on these beaches that visitors spend much of their time. These are the beaches upon which the fisherman pulls up his boat and upon which children play. However, from the point of view of their plant and animal life they seem at first to be dead, or almost so. As we shall see this is not really the case.

Sand is composed of small pieces of stone or shell and its colour depends on its origin. The pure white sands are derived from crushed coral; an admixture of shell fragments will colour the white sands yellowish or even brown. The famous black sand beaches of some of the eastern Caribbean islands are composed of tiny fragments of black volcanic rock. Sandy beaches are very varied depending mainly on the amount of wave action. Sheltered bays tend to have gently sloping beaches of fine sand, grading into mud, silt and mangrove swamp. Exposed beaches on the other hand are often steep and composed of coarse sand with perhaps stones or boulders as well and often grade into rocky or stony

Fig 3.1 Caribbean beaches are justly famous and sometimes a little crowded. However, besides all the people, there are often more animals about than you might think.

beaches. There may or may not be an offshore coral reef. Where this is present, the beach is mostly protected from large waves, as these break on the reef. This is particularly important from the conservationist point of view as clearly anything which tends to kill or destroy the offshore reef will often lead to drastic changes in the profile of the beach or perhaps to its complete disappearance. Too often ill-advised contractors have dynamited reefs without realizing the consequences of their action.

LIFE IN THE SAND

Life in sand presents problems but also confers advantages on its inhabitants. The problems relate mainly to the shifting nature of the substrate. Plants cannot attach themselves to sand and large seaweeds are absent. Animals cannot become fixed in the way that limpets and barnacles do on rocky shores or reefs. It is difficult or impossible for many animals to find homes; for example, crevice-living creatures so common under stones are not found in sand. Even the maintenance of a burrow may be difficult. The nature of the terrain means that any creature that ventures forth on the surface of the sand is clearly visible to predators; gone are the hiding places of the mangroves and the reefs. The major advantage that sand dwellers gain is, paradoxically, protection. If they can manage to survive in, rather than on, this difficult substrate then they are invisible and often beyond the reach of many predators.

Fig 3.2 Over sandy seabeds predators may abound. There is no place to hide unless you burrow into the sand, which is just what many of the inhabitants do. Here a barracuda patrols with barjack.

However, life in sandy beaches is never very rich, partly because of the difficulties and partly because the material to support the community must come in from outside. There are a few microscopic plants living on the individual sand grains, or even on the surface of the seabed in quiet places, but much of what is consumed has to be washed in from outside. Most of this material will be either plankton or detritus so that many of the inhabitants of sandy beaches are adapted to feed on small particles. Such animals usually fall into one of two categories, namely filter feeders or suspension feeders. The former create a current of water which they then sieve, collecting edible material of a particular size, other larger or smaller particles being rejected. Suspension feeders are often much more passive, simply holding out some large collecting organ or a set of sticky tentacles and catching whatever the current or wave action brings them. However, some sand dwellers feed by eating the sand and digesting what little organic matter it contains, as earthworms do with soil.

Often the only indication of life below the surface is the presence of the open mouths of burrows. Some animals such as crabs may use these burrows as homes, and venture out in search of food. For others, who may live permanently in the sand, burrows are a connection with the world above the surface through which seawater is often drawn, bringing oxygenated water and food to the inhabitant. Many bivalve molluscs live submerged in the sand but maintain an open connection with the surface by means of fleshy tubes, or siphons, through which they draw a current of water. This water passes over the fine gills bringing oxygen and removing carbon dioxide and waste. Any particles of food in the water are captured in mucus on the gills and passed to the mouth. In this way the bivalve can gain all it needs for its survival and growth without even leaving the protective sand in which it lives. These bivalves include *Donax*, sometimes called the chip-chip, which is very common on some exposed, surf-beaten beaches. This animal can be collected by hand and eaten either steamed or in soup. The shell is easy to recognize as its edge is milled like a silver coin and the small serrations can be easily felt with the fingernail. Other common sand dwelling bivalves include the pen shell, *Pinna*, which may reach 8 inches (20 cm) in length, various lucines and the elegant and colourful tellins.

Some worms may go on further than a simple burrow and build themselves a tube of sand grains cemented together with mucus into which they can retreat. Especially noteworthy are the beautiful

Fig 3.3 *Meoma ventricosa* is a large sea urchin, but unlike many of its cousins it is asymmetrical and partially flattened to suit it to its life on and in sand.

tube-building fan worms. These suspension feeders have a colourful circle of tentacles which they hold out like an upturned umbrella to catch food particles. This delicate net is rapidly withdrawn into the tube at the slightest disturbance.

Sea urchins are quite common on sandy seabeds. They include the large dark red-brown heart urchin, *Meoma*, and various species of the flattened sand dollar such as *Mellita* and *Encope*. Sand dwelling urchins feed in various ways, many of which are not well understood. In some cases they are suspension feeders, gathering up food that settles on or near them; some apparently search for food hidden in the sand while others may eat sand grains, digesting the organic matter from their surfaces. *Meoma* frequently has small crabs living in among the spines of the underside where they gain a considerable measure of protection from predators.

PREDATORS

The beautiful mollusc *Natica* lives in the sand, ploughing its way along until it encounters a bivalve when it will bore a hole through the shell and consume the unfortunate occupant. The boring of the hole takes some time and is effected by *Natica*'s rasping mouthparts aided by an acid secretion which softens the shell. It is not uncommon to find such bored shells washed up on the beach. The hole is easily identified as it gets narrower towards the inside of the shell and is usually not more than 0.25 inch (0.6 cm) diameter.

Another sand dwelling predator is the box crab *Calappa*. This crab spends most of its time hidden under the surface of the sand holding its bizarre shaped claws neatly folded against its face.

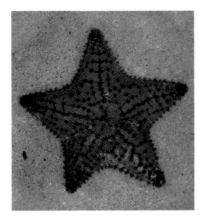

Fig 3.4 The large starfish, *Oreaster reticulatus*, is sometimes seen moving over the sandy surface in search of its favourite food, buried bivalve molluscs.

Fig 3.5 The undersurface of *Oreaster reticulatus* shows the hydraulically operated tube feet with which it walks and grips its prey. The mouth can be seen in the centre surrounded by spines.

These strong claws are used to chip open the mollusc shells on which it feeds. They are also used in defence and can deliver a very painful bite (information verified by one of the authors!).

Some starfish are specialist sand dwellers too. Best known are the members of the genera *Astropecten* and *Luidia*. These starfish differ from those living on hard substrates by having tube feet which are pointed while those of other starfish have a sucker on the end. This reflects the fact that there is nothing in their sandy environment to attach themselves to. Members of both genera feed on bivalves.

FISH

Although there is a smaller range of species of fish living on or over sandy seabeds, none the less there are a number of characteristic members of the group that are frequently encountered while snorkelling or diving. One of the most beautiful is the peacock flounder, *Bothus lunatus*. Like most of its flatfish relatives, this flounder can change colour to match its surroundings and also is frequently buried in the sand so that all that is visible are the eyes. However, if caught in the open it often displays brilliant splashes of blue against its brown ground colour. The sand tilefish maintains a

Fig 3.6 The peacock flounder spends most of its time lying on the seabed. It is difficult to see as it is usually partially covered with sand as well as being camouflaged.

burrow, usually surrounded by small stones, from which it sometimes emerges. It is a long silvery fish with a yellow face and may be up to 24 inches (60 cm) long. More often all one sees is its open mouth at the entrance to its home, a nasty surprise for small crustaceans that might be passing. The smooth trunkfish, *Lactophrys triqueter*, does not attempt to hide but swims above the sand, pausing occasionally to blow water at the substrate, presumably to uncover the small invertebrates which are its prey. Spectacular and to some extent hazardous are the stingrays. These relatives of the sharks lie hidden in the sand and are armed with spines containing toxin in their tails. If disturbed they will lash out with the tail and can deliver a painful wound to the unwary.

SAND DWELLERS ABOVE SEA LEVEL

Many marine animals have evolved over millions of years to the extent that they can make use of the boundary between sea and land. This applies to all seashore habitats. On most Caribbean sand

Fig 3.7 The ghost crab, *Ocypode*, often renews the entrance to its burrow at dusk when the tourists have given up kicking sand about.

beaches one will see the burrows of crabs above the high water mark. These burrows may be right on the beach, a little way inland or even far from the beach. There are three main types of crabs responsible for making these burrows. Those nearest the water's edge are probably the easiest to observe. Most sunbathers, if they lie quietly, will observe the appearance from such a hole of a pale-coloured active crab which runs about the sand in an effortless way almost as if blown by the wind. These ghost crabs, *Ocypode*, are tideline scavengers, difficult to catch and capable of delivering a painful pinch if cornered. If their burrows become blocked with sand, the crabs will dig their way out, energetically throwing sand some distance.

Further inland are found two common species of land crab. These are the red coloured *Ucarcinus*, and the larger grey coloured *Cardisoma*. Both are edible and as they are largely nocturnal are hunted by torchlight. In Antigua, ingenious wooden live traps are set for them. Ghost crabs are also often 'torched' for bait by fishermen.

THE TIDE LINE

Beachcombing is most rewarding on sandy beaches. Here at the high tide mark and at the water's edge one finds bits and pieces of animals and plants from deeper regions of the sea. Shells, of course,

Fig 3.8 The crabs of the genus *Uca* are known as fiddler crabs. This is because the males possess one much enlarged claw which is often moved back and forth with a 'violin-bowing' action. The claw can deliver a nasty nip but is mainly used as a signal in fights with other males and perhaps to attract females.

make up the most beautiful part of any flotsam collection. If there are coral reefs offshore or a rich sandy bay there is a real chance of finding decent specimens of the smaller conchs, star shells, small tritons, cowries, top shells and so on. Occasionally there will be a rarer musical volute or helmet shell. Sea urchin shells will also be common, often bleached white, while crab claws and lobster legs are attractively coloured in reds, blues and yellows. One great advantage of collecting in this way is that one is not killing the animal to take its shell. While any conservationist rightly deplores the taking of live molluscs for their shells, no one objects to the beachcomber collecting the many beautiful but empty shells thrown up on the sandy beaches. Plant remains, too, can be fascinating. Many seeds and fruits of land plants float in the sea and so are washed from island to island – even from continent to continent. The best known example is the coconut and at the back of undisturbed beaches their germinating fruits are frequently found. Other seeds which are not uncommon include the shiny, grey, stone-like horse-nickers and various large beans. Seaweeds also are cast up and those which are well worth collecting are the various calcareous algae. These plants lay down a skeleton composed of calcium carbonate and long after they are dead and gone the shell remains, bleached white. One of the commonest genera is *Halimeda*.

Fig 3.9 Beachcombing can be a very rewarding and informative experience. These objects were all collected from the same beach in the space of a few minutes. They include urchin tests, pieces of sponge, gastropod and bivalve shells as well as the calcareous skeletons of seaweeds.

Fig 3.10 Beware the beach thieves! These Jamaican grackles are not really shore birds but they'll take picnic out of your hand if you don't watch out.

4 Seagrass Beds

In shallow, flat-bottomed inshore waters one often finds beds of grass-like plants growing over large areas. These plants are unusual marine plants for, unlike the true seaweeds which are algae, these seagrasses (sometimes called turtle-grasses) are flowering plants. There are two main genera of Caribbean seagrass, *Thalassia* and *Diplanthera*. The latter usually grows closer inshore and can be distinguished in that beds of it look dark compared with the lighter coloured *Thalassia*. *Diplanthera* is also somewhat more tolerant of fresh water running off or through the beach. Neither can tolerate being uncovered for any length of time by the retreating tide. It is worth while making the point that in the tropics generally there is not such a rich intertidal flora and fauna and those more used to temperate regions will miss the jumbled masses of brown and red seaweeds that low tides usually reveal. There are two main reasons for this. Firstly, the relatively small tides mean that the total area covered and uncovered by each tide is small. Secondly, because of the tropical sun, the marine plants and animals of the intertidal

Fig 4.1 This sheltered bay has a seabed partially of sand (the paler areas) and partially of seagrass (the darker areas).

zone are subjected to a tremendous drying and heating influence when uncovered; few are able to survive. The low nutrient level and active herbivorous habit of many animals reduce seaweed growth even further.

Seagrasses not only have their blade-like leaves above the sand but also grow extensive underground creeping stems or rhizomes equipped with roots. As these plants only flower infrequently it is likely that dispersal is vegetative; that is by the breaking off and subsequent growth of fragments of the whole plant rather than by seeds. Indeed, in *Thalassia*, not only are flowers uncommon but all the male flowers appear at one time and all the female ones at another. Because of their rhizotomous mode of growth seagrasses bind the substrate together and give it a solidarity which is lacking in sand alone. They grow best on sand mixed with coral fragments or stones and do not thrive where the particles are all of one size. This, together with the fact that the leaves are a rich source of food, results in grass beds being habitats with a rich and varied fauna. One study of a *Thalassia* bed showed that it contained 133 species of animals (excluding fishes), 60 of them found only in turtle-grass. The nearby bare sand contained only 33 species of which 8 were found only in the sand. *Diplanthera* beds are also very rich in animal species but contain relatively few animals that are not found

Fig 4.2 Here a single plant of *Thalassia* has been dug up and displayed onshore. Leaves and roots can be seen growing from the creeping rhizome. The plant can be spread easily by fragmentation.

Fig 4.3 A general view of a seagrass bed. In the foreground is a holothurian (sea cucumber) known, for obvious reasons, as the donkey dropping sea cucumber.

elsewhere. Many of the seagrass animals live under the surface in burrows or buried in sand and they are best investigated by digging up some of the substrate and washing it through a coarse sieve with holes of approx. 0.1 inch (2 or 3 mm). (Remember, however, that this destroys the habitat and should only be done in the course of serious investigation.) In this way, one will discover a wealth of small creatures, especially small worms, crustaceans and bivalve molluscs. Particularly common among the shellfish are bivalves including the tiger lucine *Codakia* and the cross-barred venus *Chione*, and the gastropod *Prunum*, a marginella.

Where there are nooks and crannies it is not uncommon to find octopuses. These strange creatures are related to snails and bivalves and feed mainly on crustaceans. They are capable of walking over the surface of the seabed or of swimming by the rapid ejection of water from the mantle cavity, a sac-like space containing the gills. When severely frightened they will squirt out black ink that acts like a smoke screen behind which they can make their escape.

Brittlestars are also common. These are five-armed creatures related to the starfish but having much thinner more spiny arms than their cousins. They live in crannies and are suspension feeders straining out edible particles from the passing water. Very obvious in among the seagrass upon which they feed are large sea urchins. These are also related to the brittlestars and there are two common

Fig 4.4 Brittlestars (ophiuroids) are abundant in seagrass beds. They often hide under stones or pieces of dead coral during the day to avoid predation, emerging at night to filter feed. This specimen has been brought on to the sand for photographing.

Fig 4.5 The sea urchin, *Tripneustes*, grazes among the seagrass. Like a number of other urchins, it decorates itself with a variety of pieces of debris. In this case it seems to be mainly fragments of seagrass leaf that have been used but shell fragments and small stones are often used.

genera, *Tripneustes* (sea egg) and *Lytechinus*. The large white sea egg is prized in Barbados where its roes are eaten as a delicacy (though it is usually fished not in grass beds but on wave washed reefs). These urchins can be handled relatively easily unlike their relative *Diadema* whose black spines are needle sharp and can deliver a painful wound.

Fig 4.6 One of the most extraordinary inhabitants of seagrass beds is the upside-down jellyfish, *Cassiopeia xamachana*. Most jellyfish float in mid-water with their stinging tentacles hanging down but *Cassiopeia* lies in the seabed with its tentacles facing upwards.

Fig 4.7 Porcupine fish, *Diodon hystrix*, are common in seagrass beds. Like their relatives, the puffers and balloonfish, they can inflate themselves to become almost spherical. When this happens their spines project and they thus present a formidable appearance to would-be predators.

Above the seabed some more spectacular animals are to be seen. The pride of the seagrass beds, as far as the fishes are concerned, is the sea horses. These bizarre fishes are occasionally to be seen clinging to the turtle-grass by their tails. They are weak swimmers. Sometimes quite large conchs are to be found in the turtle-grass beds and smaller ones are usually common. Indeed, the grass beds are nursery grounds for many animals.

Like the mangrove swamp, the juveniles of numerous reef species are to be found here. In both places food is relatively plentiful. Very large predators are to a great extent excluded by the shallowness of the water, while there is plenty of cover in which small animals can conceal themselves. This cover is not sufficient for large animals but during the night the beds are invaded by bigger creatures, especially if there is coral nearby in which these animals can hide during the day. Thus parrotfish sally forth to eat the seagrass while grunts go in search of invertebrates and other small animals for food. This exploitation of the beds is borne out by the high density of fish on reefs close to grass beds.

Fig 4.8 Some types of sea anemones embed themselves in the substrate. Here are a group of pink-tipped anemones, *Condylactis gigantea*.

The commonest coral in turtle-grass beds is *Acropora palmata*, the elkhorn coral. In these quiet conditions the growths are often large, spreading out from a central 'stalk' like a giant table. These stands are usually isolated and are a natural gathering point for many fish.

Seagrass beds like mangrove swamps and coral reefs differ from the open ocean in being highly productive. The leaves and rhizomes of grasses are the starting point for a large and complex food web based not only on the plant material itself but also on the bacteria and moulds that bring about their decay. In contrast to most true seaweeds, which are clean and shiny, the leaves of turtle-grass are covered with a growth of minute plants and animals. A scraping from such a leaf, if examined under the microscope, reveals a whole new world. Most true seaweeds and some sedentary animals (e.g. sea fans) secrete toxic substances that prevent the accumulation of such a covering of plants and animals. Some of these substances may be of potential pharmaceutical use as antibiotics.

5 Rocky Shores

In many places in the Caribbean there is no beach and the meeting of land and sea is a rock face. Such shores, although sometimes in sheltered areas, are often pounded by ocean breakers; such is the case for the east coasts of many of the Lesser Antilles. Below the surface the animals inhabiting the rocks are in many ways similar to those of coral reefs. Indeed, if the wave action is not too great, corals may thrive on top of the rocky substrate. This chapter deals mainly with the animals and plants of the intertidal and splash zones, parts of the rocky beach which are in the open air at least some of the time. These beaches can usually be examined on foot rather than by SCUBA diving or snorkelling. However, care should be taken on these beaches as they are sometimes swept by strong waves and the rocks are often sharp and slippery.

Fig 5.1 There is a small tidal range and Caribbean seashore rocks are often soft. The result is marked erosion often accompanied by undercutting. Rocky beaches like these can be hazardous to walk on due to the extreme sharpness of the eroded stone.

Fig 5.2 Seaweeds do grow on these shores but not in the profusion seen in temperate climates. Included in this selection of rocky shore algae is the common and easily recognized *Padina* with its characteristic semicircular growth lines.

Wave-worn rocks allow the settlement of many attached animals. Some of these are fixed in one place for life; others cling on while the surf beats on their backs but can move and feed when calmer conditions permit. Into the former group fall the barnacles. These creatures are of tremendous importance on rocky shores in temperate regions but on many West Indian shores they may be hard to find. It is difficult for many people to realize that these small, shelled animals cemented to rocks are in fact relatives of the active crabs and lobsters. However, they are indeed crustaceans as has been clearly shown by investigations of their life cycle. The eggs, which are shed into the sea, develop into tiny swimming larvae that live for a while in the plankton. At this stage they have the characteristics, including jointed legs and so on, of crustaceans, but if they survive, they settle on a suitable surface and change into the adult form. They retain their jointed legs, however, which are used to capture small animals for food. Other attached species include sponges, hydroids, anemones, tunicates and tube worms.

Fig 5.3 Chitons are easily identified by their eight shell plates. This flexible armour permits them to mould to the surface tightly when out of water.

Those that hang on rather than live out their time stuck to one place are mainly molluscs: snails, limpets and chitons. The snails are mostly small and inconspicuous such as the winkles. These tiny creatures often live high above the high tide mark browsing on algae and lichen on the rock surfaces. During the day when most of us go to such places the winkles are inactive. At night, however, they are out and about. The reason for this nocturnal activity is mainly to avoid predators such as crabs and birds which may hunt by sight, and also to keep water loss by evaporation to a minimum. This loss would, of course, be particularly great in the heat of the day; indeed it is remarkable that the animals can survive the very considerable heating they must undergo on their sun-drenched rocks. Although small, these common shells have a beauty of their own. Particularly attractive is the black and white *Littorina ziczac*, the zebra winkle (for once the Latin name is more attractive than the common one).

The larger snails include the colourful and variable nerites, of which the bloody-toothed nerite, *Nerita peloronta*, is perhaps the

Fig 5.4 Tiny zebra winkles, *Littorina ziczac*, inhabit the upper part of the shore. They are seen here clustering together in depressions in the rock in order to minimize water loss during the daytime heat.

Fig 5.5 The prickly winkle, *Nodolittorina tuberculata*, is rather bigger than the zebra winkles but lives in similar places.

Fig 5.6 There are three common species of nerite to be found on rocky shores. They are seen here from both the upper and lower sides. The left hand *Nerita tesselata* is the easiest to distinguish with the black and white chequered pattern on the shell. The other two, *N. versicolor* (centre) and *N. peloronta* (right), are almost impossible to tell apart until you turn them over. Then the bright red marking of *N. peloronta* (which gives it the common name of bloody-toothed nerite) is an immediate give-away.

most spectacular. The area close to the opening of the shell is stained blood red so that its name is almost horribly appropriate. Usually, this species is found alongside another, *Nerita versicolor*, which is almost indistinguishable until turned over when the lack of the red stain identifies it. A third species, *Nerita tesselata*, with a checked black and white shell, is also commonly found in the same habitat but usually in rock pools.

The limpets are found further down the shore and may be of two basic types. These gastropods have uncoiled conical shells which are either complete or have a hole at the apex. The latter are separate from common or garden limpets and given the name key-hole limpets. As with the snails, their shells, although often small, repay careful examination. These creatures, like most of the snails, are browsers rasping the microscopic plants off the rock surfaces with a file-like tongue called the radula.

The chitons are molluscs whose shell covering is composed of eight jointed sections allowing them the flexibility to mould themselves to the rock surface and so withstand the force of the waves. So tightly can they adhere to the rocks that, if attempts are made to remove them, they often break apart before they detach. Lower

Fig 5.7 Hermit crabs are usually very common on rocky shores. When you see a winkle that runs, either it's a hermit crab or blame the rum!

down rocky shores the fauna may be more varied and more like that of the submarine world, containing crabs (especially grapsids), urchins and sea cucumbers. One of the most attractive crabs is the calico crab, *Eriphia*. Although quite small, 2 inches (5 cm) or so across, he is a striking creature. The back is brownish green but his claws are bluish above, yellow beneath and covered in chocolate brown warts. The tips of the pincers themselves are dark brown also. In the pools will be many small gobies and other fish. On constantly wetted surfaces seaweeds are often to be found in profusion, though never as many as in the temperate regions.

Rocky shores often show excellent examples of zonation, that is, the beach is divided horizontally into bands or zones each with its characteristic animals. Thus the highest zone, splashed only by spray, will contain such snails as the common prickly winkle. Lower down where the rocks are regularly wetted by the high tides come the nerites and the littorinas. Below this comes a mid-tide zone which is usually submerged for half of the time or perhaps more. Here live many limpets and the barnacles. Below this, the zones merge into the truly marine community of animals, most of which cannot tolerate even brief periods out of water. This pattern of zonation (which is found on other shores too; see for example the section on mangrove swamps in Chapter 2) varies from shore to shore but follows a fairly general pattern.

Rocky shores are ideal situations for investigation into zonation patterns by groups of naturalists or students. The high shore is especially suitable as it contains relatively few species and is usually accessible.

Fig 5.8a, b, High shore snails are easily available prey for a range of animals. Camouflage is some protection against predators that use sight to detect their prey. Here you can see the difference between the left-hand picture with the snails (*Thais patula*) on the patch of rock which they selected for themselves and the right-hand picture showing how the same snails stand out on a piece of newly fractured rock.

Fig 5.9 Rocky shores in the Caribbean are not always calm. Those facing the prevailing trade winds are often wave-swept and wild. Shores like this one on the east coast of Barbados have a broad wave-cut platform with many pools and a wide splash zone; they are a good but very hazardous place to observe rocky shore flora and fauna.

6 Coral Reefs

A coral reef is one of the most complex communities of plants and animals in the world. The richness of the flora and fauna on the reef contrasts with the relatively barren seas surrounding it. However, we should not forget that the reef is a delicate thing whose life can be destroyed by quite small changes in the surroundings. Pressures on the coral reefs of the Caribbean are growing year by year and there is an urgent need to conserve these valuable natural reserves. But for these reefs, inshore fisheries would suffer and beaches would disappear under wave action.

Reefs are a tourist attraction and many visitors regard a glass-bottomed boat trip, a snorkel or a SCUBA dive session as the highlight of their Caribbean holiday. More and more the region will be forced back to its own resources and thus we cannot afford to damage or destroy reefs. Despite this, it is unfortunately true that

Fig 6.1 The seaward edges of these fringing reefs are marked by the breaking waves. Originally the coral growth will have started in the shallow water close to land. Gradually the reef has grown seawards accumulating dead coral and other deposits in the inshore lagoon. The front faces of these reefs often plunge into deep water making the spectacular submarine cliffs so beloved of SCUBA divers.

destruction of coral reefs is taking place throughout the Caribbean. Sometimes the destruction is in the name of progress, for example deep-water harbours are built or hotels are constructed. Sometimes it is through ignorance, when the yachtsman or fisherman smashes coral with his anchor. Sometimes, also, it is cynically and knowingly done by collectors or beach developers. In some places this process of destruction is being slowed or stopped by legislation and protection but the laws are often difficult to enforce. Moreover, in a region such as the Caribbean, even conservationists must realize the existence of competing claims; for instance, a deep-water harbour may well benefit the local community a great deal. Perhaps, however, it could be constructed with the biological factors in mind. One hopes that in future governments and those in control of development will increasingly seek out and incorporate the views of conservationists into their policies.

On the constructive side there are a number of attempts now being made to create artificial reefs. This is being done by dropping wreckage and rubbish, old car bodies, tyres, even worthless hulks, into the sea at suitable depths. These objects are quickly grown over by reef organisms and become productive areas. Such projects are relatively cheap and have the dual advantage of reducing pollution on land while increasing the amenity and production potential of the sea. In all such projects care must be taken that toxic

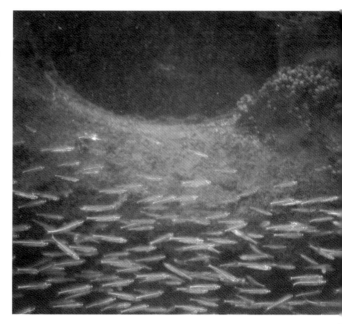

Fig 6.2 In many cases man-made structures will act as reefs, at least for many marine creatures. Sometimes these artificial structures will be put in place intentionally, sometimes by accident. Here an old car tyre is home to juvenile fish.

items are not incorporated into these reefs and that the objects used are stable enough not to be scattered on the seabed or washed ashore in storms.

CORALS

The most important creatures on the reefs are the corals themselves. Corals are animals, albeit fairly simple ones. They are closely related to sea anemones and rather more distantly to jellyfish.

Fig 6.4 This picture is really here to show what retracted coral polyps look like but the Christmas tree worm is insisting on stealing the show.

Fig 6.5 In contrast to Fig 6.4, the polyps of this star coral are seen here to be expanded with the tentacles extended so as to catch small planktonic prey. Most corals remain contracted during the day but expand at night.

Coral organisms, called polyps, are rather like tiny sea anemones in appearance with a ring of tentacles surrounding a central mouth. Most coral polyps are withdrawn during the day but extended at night. However, this is not a hard and fast rule and some coral polyps may extend in the daytime.

Corals can capture various tiny animals and plants that float in the sea. The prey animals, which are generally larger than the microscopic plants, are caught by the tentacles which are armed with tiny sting cells called nematocysts. These can be discharged explosively, throwing out threads which may both harpoon and poison the prey. (In large sea anemones, nematocysts may kill quite large fish while those of jellyfish and Portuguese man-o'-war can cause very painful and sometimes dangerous stings to man.) The coral's prey is then transferred to the mouth. This may take place by a movement of the tentacles or by the prey being swept over the surface of the coral polyp trapped in a layer of mucus. This mucus covers the whole coral and is constantly being swept towards the polyp's mouth by the action of microscopic hair-like processes on the surface of the living tissue. It often acts as a trap for tiny floating plants which are passed in through the mouth and digested. The mucus also prevents larvae of other animals settling on the coral and keeps it clean of sand and silt particles.

Large pieces of organic matter that fall on to a coral colony may be too big to be taken in through a polyp mouth. In this case digestive threads are passed out from the body cavity and surround the object,

Fig 6.6 Like all settled reef organisms, corals compete for space. Many adopt shapes which permit them to overgrow less aggressive creatures. This photograph shows a colony of *Porites asteroides* competing well.

which is slowly broken down. Animals that indiscriminately catch any floating particles in this way are termed suspension feeders because they are feeding on suspended organic matter in the water.

Death of coral may occur in a variety of ways, but one of the commonest causes is overgrowing. If two growing colonies meet, one of them tends to grow over the other. The covered coral will usually die under such conditions. Some slow-growing species protect themselves from faster growing ones by thrusting out the digestive filaments mentioned earlier. These can kill the encroaching coral. However, in recent years there has been widespread death of coral due to other causes. These are dealt with on page 141.

Some corals are composed of a single simple polyp while others are clearly colonies of many polyps. Yet other species are formed of polyps that are much deformed from the typical shape (e.g. brain corals). In colonial forms new polyps simply bud off from existing ones. We have seen that a coral polyp is like a tiny sea anemone which sits in a cup in its skeleton. This cup is not smooth inside, however, but has a knob or ridge rising from the centre of the bottom (the columella) while there are a number of flat vertical plates (the septa) coming from the outside wall towards the centre of the cup. Single-polyp corals may grow to be quite large. More usually, the polyp, as it grows, divides to form a colony. Sometimes this new polyp will form from tissue well outside the area of the mouth and tentacles. In that case the new polyps will be clearly separated, each having a separate cup. Sometimes, however, a new mouth

Fig 6.7 In the flower coral, *Eusmilia fastigiata*, the polyps are not so regularly circular as those of the star coral (Fig 6.5) but are distorted somewhat. When a polyp becomes very broad in one direction it will split into two. In this species the continual splitting leads to branched colonies.

may form within the area of the oral disc enclosed by the tentacles. In this case the new mouth may gradually grow away from the original and eventually form a new separate polyp or the separation may remain incomplete. *Eusmilia* is an example of the former type. Most specimens of this beautiful coral show polyps which are in various stages of this separation process. The latter case is shown in, for example, the brain corals. Here the oral discs surrounding the mouths never separate and the result is that the columella instead of forming a pillar takes the shape of a meandering ridge so characteristic of these corals.

Fig 6.8 Distortion of polyps away from the simple circular form reaches its extreme in brain corals (*Diploria* spp.) where the circles become convoluted grooves.

New colonies can also be produced by sexual reproduction. Eggs and sperm are released into the sea and the fertilized egg develops into a tiny swimming creature, the planula (pl. planulae). Not infrequently the fertilization of the egg is internal. The sperms are formed from ridges inside the body cavity and are shed through the mouth. Some of these sperm are taken up through the mouth of polyps containing eggs which are fertilized in the body cavity. Some development takes place inside the cavity before the now fully motile planula is released. Experiments suggest that planulae at first swim upwards and towards the light. Later, however, they sink to the seabed in search of a new home. The larval life usually lasts for only a few days after which the planula settles down and forms a tiny polyp. Many planulae are, of course, eaten as they swim in the plankton.

A remarkable thing about the coral polyp is the fact that it has living in its tissues thousands of single-celled algae (zooxanthellae). These do not harm the coral, indeed the relationship seems to be to their mutual advantage. A beneficial partnership such as this is termed a symbiosis. The zooxanthellae obtain nutrients from the waste products of the coral polyps while the corals gain from the zooxanthellae the ability to form the hard calcium carbonate skeleton that is so characteristic of stony corals. This is a complex

Fig 6.9 The flame scallop is one of the most spectacular reef bivalves. However, its scarlet mantle tentacles would look black to a diver, even at quite shallow depths, because of the poor penetration of red light through seawater. Its true colour is seen here thanks to flash photography.

process in which active photosynthesis by the zooxanthellae plays an essential part. Corals placed in the dark or whose zooxanthellae are destroyed are incapable of forming the typical skeleton. Because corals can only form their skeletons with the help of their photosynthesizing zooxanthellae it is obvious that they cannot form skeletons in dark places. Thus corals do not thrive, as do some sponges and tunicates, on the undersides of stones. Nor do they grow well where suspended silt in the water cuts out the light. Seawater itself absorbs some light and as one goes deeper and deeper so it becomes more and more gloomy, however bright the sun and clear the water. This means that corals will not grow well below a depth of about 200 feet (60 m) and even below 100 feet (30 m) the forms are relatively delicate. Massive corals are confined to shallow depths. The white sunlight is, of course, made up of light of various colours. These colours do not penetrate seawater equally. Red light especially lacks penetration, and at 65 feet (20 m) red objects look black as there is no red light for them to reflect. This is the reason why many divers are astonished when they see colour pictures taken at depths with an electronic flash unit or floodlight. For the first time perhaps they see the wealth of red tints and hues. The same effect can be obtained on a dive by taking a pressure-resistant flashlight which will supply the lost parts of the spectrum.

The process of coral growth is a relatively slow one. Although the slender branches of *Acropora cervicornis* may grow inches each year this is very rapid compared with other corals, especially very heavy solid forms such as the brain corals.

As well as being essential for coral skeleton formation the zooxanthellae contribute food to the coral. The tiny algal cells are able to capture the energy from sunlight and use it to make substances such as sugars. Some of these leak from the algae into the surrounding coral cells where, of course, they can be utilized as food.

As has been mentioned, the productivity of the reef is many times higher than that of the surrounding oceans and far higher than the nutrient levels of the seas would suggest is possible. This high productivity seems to be the result of at least two factors. Firstly, the protected zooxanthellae add considerably to the total photosynthetic capability of the reef; these algae may total three times the weight of the animal tissue of the coral. Secondly, the reef with its many different animals and plants tends to conserve its nutrients trapped within the tightly knit food webs and cycles of the reef. Little of what is produced within the reef is lost to the open sea. Thus in the water close to the reef the nutrients, detritus and zooplankton levels may be tens or hundreds of times the levels in the ocean.

The gross shape of the corals varies enormously. Perhaps the most beautiful are the delicate branching shapes of the staghorn coral, *Acropora cervicornis*. To see this coral growing in beds like miniature forests with brilliant blue chromis swimming among them is perhaps one of the most beautiful sights awaiting the SCUBA diver or snorkeller. Impressive by their very bulk are the huge spherical masses of such corals as *Siderastrea*. Many of the brain corals can also reach massive proportions and here the convoluted surface patterns add further sculptural interest. Some smaller corals have a branched finger-like appearance. Two such corals, both common, are species of *Porites* and *Madracis*. In the beautiful *Eusmilia* the branches end in an almost flower-like single polyp. For stately beauty no coral can improve on the pillars of *Dendrogyra*

Fig 6.10 The staghorn coral, *Acropora cervicornis*, forms forests of branches in shallow, relatively calm water.

Fig 6.11 Elkhorn coral, *Acropora palmata*, is an important reef builder and is a dominant coral close to the surface at the seaward edges of reefs. Both species of *Acropora* have been severely affected by disease and other problems over the last two decades and they are much less common than formerly.

which may reach up to 7 feet (2 m) in height rising from the reef like massive stalagmites.

Some corals, especially those with an extended depth range, show great individual variation of form. Perhaps the best example is *Agarica agaricites*. This coral forms knobbly lumps in shallow water but at depths of 100 feet (30 m) or so it takes the form of delicate flat plates. Generally speaking corals are more delicate at depths below 80 feet (25 m). This is in part due to the low light intensity which reduces the photosynthesis of the zooxanthellae upon which skeleton formation is dependent. However, it may also be that heavier skeletal formations are an adaptation to the more turbulent water conditions nearer the surface.

Fig 6.12 The club finger coral, *Porites porites*, is to be found even in very shallow water as well as in isolated patches in seagrass beds.

Fig 6.13 Flat plate-like growth of coral is often found on the steep seaward side of reefs.

Fig 6.14 All corals, soft and stony, use their polyps to catch drifting prey. This flash photograph shows the water packed with particles including plankton, some of which will be food for the polyps.

Fig 6.15 The star coral, *Montastrea annularis*, often forms large domed structures as much as 7 feet (2 m) across.

The ability to form a hard skeleton, which will persist after the polyp dies, means that coral growth over the years can form solid rocky structures of very considerable size. The upper portions of these are, of course, the reefs themselves. Reefs may form in various ways and in various places. Different types of reef have often been given names such as fringing, patch, barrier, bank, etc. However, there is not always agreement about the use of these names and many reefs do not have a simple structure fitting one or other of the types. None the less the reefs of the Caribbean can mostly be classified into one of three main categories described below.

- **Fringing reefs**   These are the most usual type of reef in the West Indies. They are formed by coral establishing itself in the relatively shallow water at the edge of the shore and then gradually growing outwards into the sea. Such reefs come close to the surface of the water at their seaward edge and indeed waves may break on them. As the growth pushes out to sea the shore side of the reef tends to die and the dead coral compacts down to form a lagoon where depth may vary from a few to many feet. This lagoon may become filled with sand and support turtle-grass beds (see page 38). The front side of such a reef may fall steeply into deep water giving spectacular underwater scenery. The action of waves may erode gullies of considerable depth in the front face of such reefs. In other places similar gullies contain sand which gradually overflows from the lagoon.

  Smaller gullies are often found in shallow water. They are cut in towards the shore and may have sandy bottoms. This type of underwater contouring is known as spur and groove, and is particularly attractive as the steep sides of the spurs form coral cliffs (although they may be only 3 or 4 ft or so high).

  Each part of the reef has its own characteristic corals. For instance, the zone where the waves are breaking is often rich in elkhorn coral while the deeper front face of the reef has much of the more delicate staghorn coral.

- **Barrier reef**   This is a term which is sometimes used for fringing reefs which have formed parallel to a shore but with a fairly wide space between the shore and the shallow reef front. However, the term is best reserved for huge reefs found many miles off continental landmasses, e.g. the Great Barrier Reef off the east coast of Australia. In the Caribbean the best example is the barrier reef off the coast of Belize. This lies about 9 miles

(15 km) off the coast and varies in width from 6 to 20 miles (10 to 32 km). The central and most spectacular section contains 57 miles (91 km) of almost continuously developed barrier reef with numerous lagoons containing seagrass beds and sand cays as well as patch reefs and mangrove islands.

- **Patch reefs** These reefs may develop in water of medium depth on relatively flat sea bottoms if suitable conditions exist. Reef structure is made more complicated by the fact that during the geological history the sea level in the Caribbean has not been constant and many landmasses have either risen or sunk. Thus in Barbados one can easily see a succession of reefs that have been lifted up one after the other out of the sea. It is possible to interpret the vast areas of coral in the Bahamas as essentially a huge collection of patch reefs that have developed in this region of shallow sea.

The building of coral reefs is not only brought about by corals themselves. Many seaweeds also form stony deposits and most importantly some coralline algae grow over coral debris cementing the loose pieces together to produce a solid firm substrate for further growth.

If one has the opportunity to examine a piece of coral rock, that is to say a fragment of a former reef perhaps hundreds of thousands of years old, one can see the many components. As well as the coral itself there is much compacted sand together with the skeletons of many marine animals and plants, especially molluscs, echinoderms and coralline algae. There may also be a sizeable contribution of foraminiferan shells. These tiny unicellular animals usually form a calcareous shell often like that of a minute mollusc. Although they seldom exceed 0.04 inch (1 mm) in size their huge numbers may make then important in reef formation.

Destructive forces are also at work in the reef. You will see in almost any piece of dead coral you collect on the beach a variety of holes and tunnels. These are produced by animals which bore into the coral to create homes for themselves. Investigations have shown that commonly 10 per cent or more of the coral skeleton is destroyed in this way. Much dead coral is ground into sand and washed away to the seabed or beaches.

The living coral, upon which the whole community depends, is a sensitive creature and changes in salinity, light and silt levels and some pollutants can result in the death of the reef. Although regeneration can occur it is slow indeed, as is the growth of the coral itself.

Many measurements of the ages of corals have been made and the smaller species seem to average 7 years old (some species take this long to reach sexual maturity). An Australian colony has been aged at 140 years but the larger West Indian species, especially those of the massive dome-like *Diploria* and *Montastrea*, may be far older than this. Growth rates of just over 0.4 inch (1 cm) per year seem to be typical for these colonies and as many of them are over 7 feet (2 m) in diameter this would make them over 200 years old.

This section has dealt with the creatures we call 'coral'. However, this is a broad term which is also applied to related organisms. Reef building corals which produce a calcium carbonate skeleton are technically known as the Scleractinia or stony corals. We will consider some of the other 'corals' in the following sections. The commonest of these are the fire corals.

FIRE CORALS

These creatures belong to a group called the Hydrocorallina. Their polyps protrude from the limy skeleton and can be seen with the naked eye as fine hair-like filaments. In fact, there are two distinct types of polyps. Those that are visible appear to act as guards or touch sense organs. They have no mouth but carry short stinging tentacles along their length. The second type of polyp is much short-er and fatter. It has a mouth with four stinging tentacles around it. These are the polyps that capture and ingest the food which is small planktonic creatures and particles of organic matter. Inside the skeleton all the polyps are connected by a net of delicate tubes.

Fire coral is so-called because of the burning sting it can deliv-er if touched. Many unwary snorkellers have attempted to collect a piece with their bare hands, something they only try once. It is the guard polyps which are mainly responsible for this sting.

The gross form of the fire corals is very varied. They tend to grow over objects; divers sometimes find discarded bottles that have been beautifully decorated in this way. In disturbed water the colonies may be rather stout, broad fans. In quieter waters the form may be much more delicate forming an elaborate filigree on the reef. On close examination the skeleton can easily be distinguished from the true corals by the lack of the typical rayed depression of the coral polyps. Instead the relatively smooth surface is peppered with minute holes of two sizes, the smaller barely visible to the

Fig 6.16 Fire corals, *Millipora* spp., have a hard skeleton but are only distantly related to the true corals. Beware touching these growths as they can deliver the burning sting which gives them their name.

naked eye. The larger house the feeding polyps while the guard polyps protrude from the smaller holes.

THE SOFT CORALS

We have seen how the hard, stony corals are the reef builders. However, the soft corals also play an important role in the reef community.

Sea whips, sea plumes, and sea fans comprise the major groups of soft corals. These all belong to the group Alcyonaria and have a structure that bears some similarities to their stony cousins. They are all colonies of small polyps borne on a skeleton, but this is usually horny with little or no calcium carbonate. Soft corals are pliant and

Fig 6.17 Black corals, *Antipathes* spp., are also not closely related to true corals. Most live at considerable depths and in some islands may be relatively uncommon due to their having been harvested so that their polished skeletons could be made into jewellery. Fortunately this practice is declining. This picture also shows whip corals.

can bend with the currents and waves. They feed at all times of the day and night, the tentacled polyps capturing food particles from the sea. Soft corals are fastened firmly to the bottom. They add grace and beauty to the undersea world, and should not be removed.

Both the soft and hard corals provide needed shelter and food for a great many marine creatures. One of the most beautiful groups of species, the black corals, grows only in deeper waters. They are frequently seen to provide a home for the colourful sponges that fasten to the bases, countless brittlestars and other organisms.

Fig 6.18 Sea fans, *Gorgonia* spp., are one of a number of related groups generally known as soft corals.

Fig 6.19 More soft corals bend with the current.

Fig 6.20 Soft coral polyps are truly spectacular. The relationship to the true corals is not difficult to see (compare with Fig 6.5).

THE SPONGES

Other soft creatures that adorn the coral reefs include the sponges. The species found here are not the household variety, and are therefore of no commercial value.

Each sponge, no matter what its shape or size, is a living colony of single cells. The sponge 'feeds' by drawing water into its millions of microscopic chambers, straining out plankton, and ejecting the

Fig 6.21 Large basket sponges, *Xestospongia muta*, are sadly fairly rare. If you find one they certainly make for exciting diving.

Fig 6.22 The range of shapes and colours to be found in sponges is amazing.

filtered water through the large holes that are seen easily with the naked eye.

Sponges are very primitive. They belong to the group known as Porifera, and basically they have evolved very little from their pre-historic ancestors. The largest species found in the Caribbean are the basket sponges, so big at times that two human beings could sit inside one. At the other extreme, the encrusting sponges are small colonies found covering the corals or the roofs and walls of under-sea caves. Sponges support themselves with thousands of tiny spicules made of protein, silica or calcium carbonate.

If you remove a living sponge from the sea its bad smell will soon cause you to wish you hadn't! So beautiful and colourful are the sponges that they should be left in their natural habitat, where they can be viewed by divers or riders in a glass-bottomed boat. Some sponges are capable of giving a very painful sting to the unwary diver or snorkeller. These include the aptly named do-not-touch-me and fire sponges. Most stinging sponges are red in colour and to be on the safe side it is best not to touch any red sponge as the toxin-laden spicules of the stingers can spoil a day or two of your holiday or diving trip. It should also be noted by the diver that, because seawater absorbs colour, red usually appears either maroon or black at depths of more than 16 feet (5 m).

Sponges play an important part in the reef community. Like the corals, they act as a refuge for small fish, starfish, shrimp and other tiny creatures. The strange phenomenon of the 'smoking sponges' can be viewed at times by divers. This happens when sexually reproducing sponges emit clouds of sperm and eggs into the water, resembling smoke. Sponges also reproduce asexually by fragmentation and budding.

THE SPINY-SKINNED ECHINODERMS

Echinoderms all have some type of internal skeleton and often show a five-rayed symmetry. There are five major groups: the primitive crinoids or feather stars; starfish; brittlestars; sea urchins; and sea cucumbers.

- **The feather stars (crinoids)** are relatively uncommon. They are most often seen clinging to the reef or rock surface. They usually have ten feathery arms which are adapted for sieving out small food particles from the passing seawater. One of the commoner genera is *Nemaster*.

- **Starfish (asteroids)** are perhaps commoner on sandy seabeds but a number of species occur on reefs. One of the commonest

Fig 6.23 Crinoids are echinoderms. Some are more or less firmly attached to the rocks or coral. This one is more mobile and able to swim by waving its feathered arms.

Fig 6.24 In contrast to swimming crinoids, this one (*Nemaster*) usually stays put.

is *Echinaster sentus*. This five-armed starfish is covered in small, widely spaced spines and varies in colour between deep red and purple. The comet starfish (*Linckia guildingii*) takes its name from the fact that it is often found with one long and four or five short arms. This is the result of an arm being broken off a fully-grown animal which then regenerates new but smaller arms back to the normal complement of five or six. It is also reddish or purple but lacks the spines of *Echinaster*.

- **The brittlestars (ophiuroids)** also usually have five arms but unlike the starfish these are thin, spiny and attached at the centre to a small fleshy disc. Most of the Caribbean species live under stones or in crevices in the reef but some are not infrequently found in the open. *Ophiothrix* spp. are usually encountered clinging to sponges or sea fans, using their sticky tube feet to catch passing food organisms. The bizarre basket star, *Astrophyton muricatum*, is also found clinging to sponges and sea whips. This animal has an extraordinary appearance as the five arms branch again and again to produce a tangled mass often quite brightly coloured and as much as 3 feet (1 m) across.

- **The sea urchins** are very common on most reefs. The most familiar is the long-spined black *Diadema antillarum*. This creature rasps the surface of dead coral and rocks, eating the algae

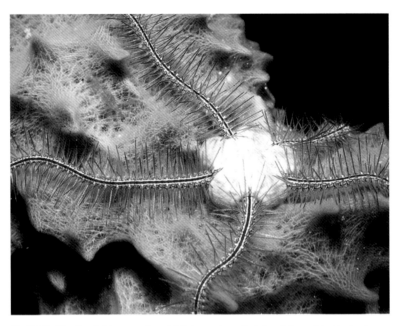

Fig 6.25 The five-fold symmetry which is so characteristic of the echinoderms is clearly seen in this brittlestar.

and other small creatures. Its spines are many inches long and needle sharp, being mainly composed of a single calcium carbonate crystal. The spines can penetrate deep into the flesh of an unwary foot or hand where they break off leaving a painful wound, made worse by the fact that the spines contain a mild toxin. The traditional West Indian treatment in such cases is the application of lime juice, but many hold that rum taken internally is almost as good! The forest of spines may sometimes serve as a refuge for small fish. In some islands, especially Barbados, the roes of the white sea egg, *Tripneustes ventricosus*, are eaten as a delicacy. These animals thrive on surf swept reefs and in turtle-grass beds. Other common urchins include the red-black or green species of *Echinometra*, which bore depressions in rocks and dead coral, and the beautiful pencil urchin, *Eucidaris tribuloides*, with its thick stubby spines.

- **The sea cucumbers (holothurians)** are soft-bodied, sausage-shaped echinoderms. These animals have a much reduced skeleton. The reef species are usually small, perhaps 4 inches (10 cm) or so long and live in nooks and crannies or under stones. Seagrass beds are the more usual habitat for members of this group.

WORMS OF THE REEF

The worms that have many bristles on their bodies are the polychaetes. They are all marine and, ironically, include some of the most beautiful creatures on the reef. Worms of the sea fall into four basic categories according to their living habits: free swimming; free crawling; tube dwelling; and burrowing. This last category has many representatives on the soft seabed, but of course they are well

Fig 6.26 The bristle worms which are found on coral reefs are often brightly coloured like this *Hermodice carunculata*.

Fig 6.27 Sabellid worms like these live in tubes. The ring of tentacles around the mouth is extended out of the tube in the form of an inverted cone. This structure catches small food particles from the water and passes them to the mouth. Should the worms sense danger the colourful tentacles are withdrawn very fast indeed.

hidden from our view. The free-swimming worms are very small, spending their lives among the plankton.

Of the crawling variety perhaps the most significant on our reefs is the fire worm. It has rows of glass-like bristles down both sides of its body, a perfect defence mechanism. Anyone or anything touching them receives a painful sting.

The most spectacular worms on the reef, and the easiest to see, are the tube-dwelling sabellids and serpulids. Often called feather dusters, the sabellids live in flexible tubes which they secrete. The smaller species often live clustered together giving the impression of a bouquet of flowers each about 0.8 to 1.2 inches (2 or 3 cm) across. The 'blossom' is actually a ring of tentacles used by the worm to trap floating food particles. Larger species are more usually solitary and may be up to 4 inches (10 cm) across. These beautiful animals would appear to be rather vulnerable to having their tentacles eaten but touch one and you will see the lightning withdrawal of the worm and its tentacles into the tube. The tentacles not only respond to touch and vibrations but also are light sensitive; if a shadow passes over the crown it often produces the withdrawal response.

One of the serpulids has been named the Christmas tree worm, *Spirobranchus giganteus* (Fig 6.4, page 54). Each one lives in a secreted tube that penetrates the coral. This worm has a twin gill, two spiralled plumes which, like the feather duster's gills, act as both a breathing and a feeding device, straining plankton and food particles from the water. At the slightest disturbance, these plumes disappear suddenly inside the tube.

The flatworms belong to a quite different and more primitive group than the polychaetes. One of the commonest species in the Caribbean is *Pseudoceros paradalis*, a truly remarkable animal, basically black with bright yellow blotches to its centre and white dots around the margin. Divers and snorkellers are most likely to find it under stones.

THE JOINTED-LEGGED ANIMALS

The marine creatures which have jointed legs are called crustaceans. They include reef dwellers like the crabs, lobsters and shrimps. They are characterized by hard, jointed outer skeletons, antennae and claws. The most popular member of this group locally is the West

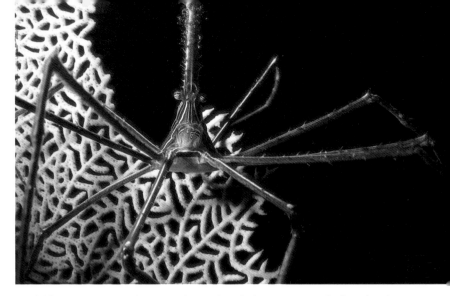

Fig 6.28 The arrow crab, *Stenorhynchus seticornis*, is a common crab of coral reefs but not always easy to see.

Indian langouste. However, a large variety of crabs and shrimps inhabit the reefs as well.

Many species of crabs occur on or near the reef. The most spectacular is probably the brightly coloured arrow crab, *Stenorhynchus seticornis*. This tiny spindly crab has a white or brown back lined in darker colours, blue claws and legs spotted or banded in red. It is sometimes found with wisps of seaweed attached to its long pointed 'nose' possibly acting as either a food store or camouflage, or perhaps both. The sponge crabs, *Dromidia*, are more difficult to see for they have a piece of living sponge on their backs. This is usually hollowed out to fit the shape of the shell and held in position by an upturned pair of legs. If upon turning over a stone you see a piece of sponge apparently walking away you can be fairly sure it is one of these strange creatures. The swimming crabs, *Portunus* spp., are handsome and wide shelled. As their name implies, they swim strongly, using the flattened end of their last pair of legs as oars. These crabs are active hunters even catching live fish. They often show differences between the two claws, one being a light slender catching claw and the other a stronger crusher. The stone crabs, *Menippe*, are much more heavily built with massive black claws. In some places these crabs are eaten and often the fishermen break off the claws returning the crab to the sea where such clawless individuals often grow new claws. They have a roughened area inside their claw which when the crab rubs it against the shell produces a characteristic noise.

Hermit crabs are very common on the reef. These, unlike the true crabs, have a soft abdomen which is adapted for clinging inside discarded snail shells. If touched, the crabs will retreat into their home blocking the entrance with the larger of their claws. There are a number of species, the commonest of which belong to the genus *Pagurus*. Snapping shrimps are not uncommon under sea anemones. These little crustaceans have dissimilar but quite heavily built claws, and are able to produce a characteristic clicking noise with the larger one.

Fig 6.29 This hermit crab has chosen the shell of a Caribbean top shell, *Cittarium pica*, as its home.

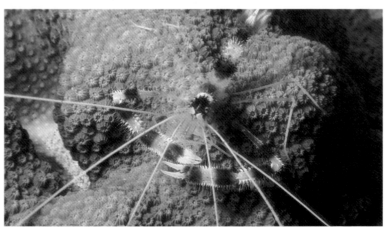

Fig 6.30 The banded coral shrimp, *Stenopus hispidus*, cleans fish of their parasites, advertising this service by waving its long, slender antennae.

While our reefs do not contain any species of shrimp large enough for the table, there exist a host of brightly coloured but very small shrimps, some of which have a most important role in the reef community. These are the 'cleaner shrimps' which remove parasites from the bodies of fish (see page 106). The largest member of this group is the banded coral shrimp with its red and white armbands. Its long white antennae, emerging from beneath a coral overhang, invite clients who need to be 'cleaned'. Some shrimp species live with anemones in the interesting relationship described on page 107.

The West Indian langouste or spiny lobster, *Panulirus argus*, was at one time plentiful in many parts of the Caribbean. However, over the years heavy fishing has depleted the stocks. It is a rare sight indeed to see the 2 feet, 30 pound (60 cm, 15 kg) monsters that must have been relatively common. The lobsters caught today average only about 3 to 4 pounds.

The adult animal is a splendid sight, varying in colour from greenish brown to dark red and having a spiny carapace and long antennae. The animal can walk over the seabed using its legs or it can swim rapidly backwards by powerful curling movements of the

Fig 6.31 The spiny lobster, *Panulirus argus*, is delicious and much in demand with both residents and visitors. Due to over-exploitation their numbers have decreased and although many Caribbean countries attempt to regulate their lobster fisheries, policing the regulations is often difficult.

abdomen which has a broad tail. It is the muscles of the abdomen that are the gourmets' delight. This animal lacks the massive claws of its cousins from northern waters but it does have large mandibles which are used for grinding up a variety of shelled animals. A Jamaican study showed that they mainly eat bivalve molluscs and also some crustaceans, plants and possibly fish. It is likely that they eat sea urchins too, where these are available. They seem to feed only at night.

Lobsters breed all the year round in the Caribbean but mating is most frequent between February and August. They are able to breed when they are about 6 inches (15 cm) or longer overall and an average female may produce 850,000 eggs. When these have been fertilized they are held under the female's abdomen for about 4 weeks, at the end of which time they hatch to release tiny larval lobsters. These live first of all in the plankton, and later in seagrass beds, mangrove swamps and under floating objects. There seem to be many stages in the larval life; growth is achieved by a succession of moults, the hard shell being incapable of stretching. This pre-adult life may take up to a year to complete and at the end of it the young lobster will be perhaps 2 inches (5 cm) long. It will probably be 2 years old before it can breed. During its adult life it continues to shed its skin every 90 days or so adding probably less than half an inch to its length each time. It is likely that large specimens are 10 years old and it takes probably 3 to 4 years to reach the minimum marketable size.

The lobster has many enemies. Its young stages are eaten by fish, especially snappers, while the adults are taken by skate, nurse sharks, groupers, octopuses, dolphins and loggerhead turtles. In view of that, it is not surprising that relatively few survive to maturity. Equally it is not surprising that intensive fishing of the adults has resulted in depletion of stocks, reduced catches and small average sizes.

In many parts of the Caribbean legislation has been passed to control the minimum size of animal caught and there is often a closed season to allow breeding to take place (and also, perhaps more importantly, to reduce the numbers of lobsters caught). It is also often illegal to take females carrying eggs. Unfortunately, all too frequently this legislation is either inadequate or unenforceable and there is no doubt that some areas have been virtually 'fished out'. Efforts are being made around the world to breed lobsters in captivity but although this has been achieved in one or two cases the cost at present makes it uneconomic even for this vastly expensive delicacy. The only answer to our problem today seems to be stricter, better enforced laws, combined with an effort to educate those responsible for the over-exploitation.

MOLLUSCS

Molluscs are those marine creatures whose beautiful, intricate, and often colourful shells are most often found on the beaches. The shelled molluscs are divided into two main groups: those in the first group have a single shell which often shows coiling – this group includes the snails; those in the second group have two shells joined together by a ligament – these are the bivalves and the group includes the clams and tellins. The living or recently dead bivalve specimen has both shells but often they come apart after death and the beachcomber will more frequently find only single valves. The molluscs also include the sea slugs, squids and octopuses which have either no shell or one which is much reduced and may be internal. Many molluscs are found in habitats other than the reef itself but we will deal with them all here for convenience.

Shells come in a great variety of shapes. Of the snails, the simplest are the almost conical limpets which cling to rocks around the low tide mark and below. Some are found to have a slit in the apex of the shell and are called keyhole limpets. Of a more typical snail-like appearance are the common West Indian top shells. These spirally wound shells are blotched black and white on the outside and are lined with iridescent mother-of-pearl. Large specimens may be 4 inches (10 cm) across. Another very attractive top shell is the chocolate-lined top shell, *Calliostoma javanicum*, which is very straight-sided and pointed with extremely regular whorls.

Some snails have a proboscis or siphon that they hold out in front of them as they move. This is essentially a sensory organ. The shells of snails with such a structure have a siphonal canal at the anterior end of the opening. Such snails include the murexes, conchs and tritons. The former have shells richly ornamented with spines and ribs while the latter two groups are among the most beautiful of West Indian shells. Murexes, such as *Murex pomum*, are commonly found in mangrove swamps while conchs and tritons more usually occur on soft seabeds.

In the cowries and their relatives, the aperture to the shell becomes large and slit-like as the shell grows and in the adult state

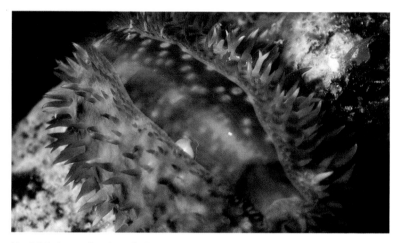

Fig 6.32 In cowries the soft, fleshy mantle is expanded out of the shell and wraps around the dorsal side. In the case of this measle cowrie, *Cypraea zebra*, the mottled brown shell is visible between the folds of the mauve mantle.

it stretches the full length of the ventral side. In life the soft part of the animal frequently spreads out almost enclosing the shell. In the flamingo tongue, *Cyphoma*, the skin of this soft tissue is pigmented orange with numerous black rings. This striking animal can often be found feeding on soft corals especially sea fans.

Another attractive group of snails is the cones. These have a long aperture set in a conical shell. The coiled spine part is often low or almost flat. These snails are predators of fish and other active animals which are killed by a toxin injected through the specialized radula tooth. Some Pacific species have killed collectors who handled them carelessly.

Fig 6.33 The flamingo tongue, *Cyphoma gibbosum*, is a mollusc commonly found on sea fans. Like the cowries the mantle almost entirely covers the shell and it is this (not the shell) which gives the spotted appearance.

Bivalve molluscs mostly live below the low tide mark either buried in mud or sand or else attached to coral or rock. A few species, including mussels such as *Brachidontes*, live firmly attached to rocks in the intertidal or splash zones. In mangrove swamps there are many oysters anchored to the roots. Shells washed up on beaches include the beautiful ribbed venuses and the smooth, colourful tellins. Perhaps the most spectacular bivalve shells come from the pen shells, *Pinna*. These translucent amber-coloured shells are triangular in shape and up to 8 inches (20 cm) long.

One need not be a diver to observe the common chiton. These molluscs belong to a group of their own separated from the bivalves and snails and have a shell composed of eight hard plates surrounded by a leathery mantle. They cling tenaciously to rocks in the intertidal zone.

Sometimes the shells of dead snails are used as homes for hermit crabs which as they grow must continually seek larger and larger shells.

Fig 6.34 Nudibranchs are (like terrestrial slugs) shell-less gastropods. They are extremely diverse in form and colour but always a joy to the eye.

◆ *The conch and its relatives*

There are about fifty recognized species of conch. Around the Caribbean the queen conch, *Strombus gigas*, is quite abundant and among the largest of the marine snails. Like other shelled creatures, it eats, reproduces, and contains a heart, stomach and a brain. Its stalked eyes peer from the shell curiously as it lies in seagrass beds, on the shallow, sandy bottom in the flats or near coral formations. The queen conch crawls about the substrate in true snail fashion, but it is also capable of hopping. The snail raises its shell with its strong, muscular foot and hooked operculum (a hard appendage that acts as a trap door to protect the soft animal when it withdraws inside the shell) and thus lurches across the sand. The immature conch is called a 'pink roller'. It does not have the full, flared lip of the mature snail and is therefore less stable on the seabed. This conch is sought after as food throughout the Caribbean. Conch steaks, fritters, salads and chowder are among the delicacies derived from this giant snail, and its shell is often used for jewellery. Like the lobster, however, the conch is endangered for the very reason that it is so popular. Unless restrictions are forthcoming that limit the taking of this marine animal, the future does not look bright for its continued existence in large numbers.

Fig 6.35 Like the spiny lobster, the queen conch, *Strombus gigas*, is much sought after for food. As a result numbers have declined dramatically in recent decades.

Fig 6.36 The queen conch only develops its wing in maturity. The younger wingless shells are called rollers. This photograph shows a roller in the centre, a young adult with a thin wing (left) and an older adult with its heavily developed wing (right).

Other species of conch include the fighting conch with its beautiful deep-orange shell and the rooster tail conch in which the outer lip has a long extension stretching far beyond the top of the spine.

The queen conch has one of the most spectacular shells in the Caribbean but no less beautiful are the helmet shells, *Cassis*, and the trumpet triton, *Charonia*. The helmets feed on sea urchins and their heavy shells are much in demand by collectors. All of these snails will be in danger of depletion or local extinction unless in some way they are protected from professional and amateur collectors who take them alive to ensure shells in prime condition.

◆ *Molluscs and food*

When a growing animal feeds, probably less than one-tenth of what it eats is incorporated into its own body, the rest is either excreted or burnt up to supply energy. In the open sea the phytoplankton is eaten by zooplankton which in turn is consumed by larger animals including small fish. These are eaten by bigger fish which are perhaps finally eaten by a 'top' predator. It is these top predators, tuna, kingfish, marlin, swordfish and so on, that constitute a large proportion of the fish caught in the Caribbean. If this fish is the result of perhaps five stages in a food chain and if 90 per cent of the material is lost at each stage, then it can be seen that the flesh of the top predator represents a vast amount of phytoplankton. From the point of view of food production it would be much more efficient to harvest either the phytoplankton itself or some animal much lower down the food chain.

Many molluscs, especially the bivalves, fit this requirement well. They mostly feed by filtering the water in which they live to obtain their food, the filter being composed of modified gills and designed to trap particles of small size, typically phytoplankton and small pieces of detritus. Because of their relatively sedentary nature (only a few can move to any extent) they use relatively little of their food for energy production and their conversion of food to flesh is very efficient. Further, their food is brought to them by the sea; they do not need to move about to collect it and as a result they can live very close together. Given all these features, it is not surprising that the production per acre of seabed by bivalves can, in suitable circumstances, far exceed that of cattle being grazed on pastures.

In various places in the Caribbean bivalves are collected and eaten. The chip-chip of Trinidad is one such but more important are the mangrove oysters *Crassostrea rhizophorae* and the mussel *Purna purna* which is collected and sold in many parts of the Caribbean. In many parts of the world bivalves are farmed by aquaculture. The extent of the encouragement given to the molluscs varies from place to place. It may be simply that a suitable place for growth is supplied or that young shells are brought from one place to seed another. At the other extreme the whole of the egg and larval stages may be passed under closely controlled conditions in a laboratory which sells the young shells (spat) for seeding.

A number of attempts are being made in the Caribbean to encourage the aquaculture of bivalves. Some involve local animals known to be of commercial importance (mangrove oysters); others involve fast growing animals such as the oyster, *Crassostrea gigas*, being imported from outside the region in the form of spat. There are also investigations being carried out on local animals which are not at present eaten but which may be useful in the future, not necessarily for human consumption but perhaps as an animal feed supplement. Such animals include the small mussel *Brachidontes* which feeds mainly on detritus stirred up in the surf on many beaches. Perhaps it could be persuaded to eat detritus from land plants, e.g. sugar cane leaves.

COMMON FISH OF THE REEFS

So great is the number of fish species found in the Caribbean waters that there is scarcely room on these pages to list them all. Some common fish families, their behaviour patterns and their role in the ecosystem, are covered here. As with the coverage of the molluscs, we will deal with most of the fishes here despite the fact that a few of them are not truly reef fish.

- **The parrotfishes** are herbivores but usually they eat plant life by chewing on hard corals and digesting the encrusting algae and zooxanthellae. They will also eat seagrass if it is available. Parrotfishes are distinctive in that their teeth form a pair of beak-like dental plates. These grind up the algal food with the soft coral rock; the latter is excreted by the fish in the form of sand. In this way the parrotfishes contribute an enormous amount of sediment to the sea bottom – over 2 tons of sand per acre, per year. These fish have many colourful species, one example being the stoplight parrot, the female of which is bright red on the underside and fins while the male is predominantly green with three diagonal orange bands on the upper half of the head.

Fig 6.37 This photograph taken on a night dive shows a stoplight parrotfish, *Sparisoma viride*, asleep on a sponge.

Fig 6.38 Grunts, *Heamulon* spp., are common in even quite shallow water and are easily seen by snorkellers.

- **The snappers** are one of the most important fish families, being sought after as food. Larger species are found in deep water. Snappers are carnivores, feeding on crustaceans and small fish. A common inhabitant of shallower reefs is the yellowtail snapper with its broad lateral yellow band, and the mangrove snapper with its faint white vertical stripes.

- **The grunts** are very similar to the snappers and are usually found in large aggregations on the reefs. The grunts are named from the strange sounds they produce by grinding their upper and lower teeth together. Collecting in small schools by day, the grunts are protected from predators. At night, they disperse to feed individually among the reefs.

Fig 6.39 Squirrelfish, *Holocentrus rufus*, and their relatives tend to be nocturnal, hiding away in small caves in the reef during the day. Their large eyes are an adaptation to this way of life. None the less, they are a common sight for most divers and snorkellers.

- **Squirrelfishes** are also nocturnal feeders. They are a very spiny family of fishes with large black eyes and red coloration. During the day, they find a niche or overhang where they remain for protection. Although squirrelfish are seen commonly in shallow waters, there are some species that exist as deep as 330 feet (100 m). Squirrelfish are generally good to eat and are often taken in fish traps set on reefs.

- **Goatfishes** are distinct from other inshore fish families in that they possess pairs of long barbels protruding from their chins. Goatfish live in close association with the sand or mud bottom; when they feed, the barbels which have sensory organs on them move rapidly over the bottom and are thrust deep into the sediment. The goatfish feed on small invertebrates beneath the sand.

- **The surgeonfishes** derive their name from sharp spikes at the base of their tails which can ward off attackers. These fish graze on algae: they are either blue (tangs) or brown (doctorfish) in colour, and are often seen in schools.

- **The groupers**, which are members of the sea-bass family, are a valuable food fish throughout the islands. The most common is the Nassau grouper, which sports zebra stripes. These fish are carnivores, feeding on fish and crustaceans. Where spearfishing has not been carried on, groupers can be tamed and hand-fed. Although they are usually seen singly, at certain times they come together for mating. For conservation reasons it is particularly important not to harass or catch fish at these mating congregations.

Fig 6.40 Goatfish, including this yellow goatfish, *Mulloidichthys martinicus*, hunt for prey in the sandy seabed in lagoons or between reefs.

Fig 6.41 Big groupers are not as common as they used to be, due in part to spearfishing. Only when this is effectively banned is there much chance of these impressive fish growing to their full size. Here we see a resting Nassau grouper, *Epinephelus striatus*.

Fig 6.42 The queen triggerfish, *Balistes vetula*, is one of the most beautiful of all Caribbean reef fish.

- **The triggerfish** has three dorsal spines which are used to threaten predators. If pursued it seeks shelter in a small recess with a restricted entrance, and raises the first dorsal spine, thus wedging itself firmly in place. In spite of their small mouths, many triggerfish feed on larger, well-armoured invertebrates such as crabs, shellfish and sea urchins. They use their powerful jaws and sharp teeth to break the animals into small pieces. The most beautiful member of this family is the queen trigger with its bright blue markings.

- **The angelfishes** cannot be rivalled for sheer beauty and grace. Deep-bodied and highly compressed, they have slender brush-like teeth, and feed primarily on sponges. Largest are the black angels, sometimes called the greys, and the French angels. Most colourful is the shy, blue and yellow queen angel. A close relative, the rock beauty, is striking with its black and yellow body. The French and black angelfishes are tame, and can easily be trained to eat from a diver's hand.

Fig 6.43 French angelfish – juvenile. (See also page 90.)

Fig 6.44 French angelfish – intermediate stage. (See also page 90.)

Fig 6.45 French angelfish – adult.

The three photographs (shown on page 89 and above) illustrate the changes in appearance which take place as the French angelfish, *Pomacanthus paru*, grows to maturity. Juveniles are stridently marked with yellow and black (Fig 6.43). Intermediate stages (Fig 6.44) show some signs of vertical stripes but also have a gold edging to the body scales while mature fish (Fig 6.45) show only the gold scale edging. (See page 100 for a possible reason for these colour changes.)

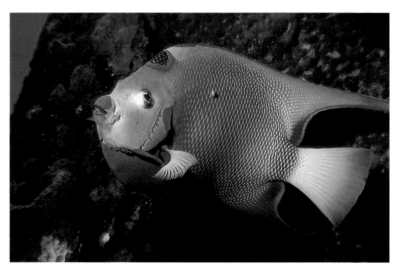

Fig 6.46 The queen angelfish, *Holacanthus ciliaris*, is probably the most spectacular member of the group.

- **The butterflyfishes** are closely related to the angelfishes. They are small in size but also deep bodied and are usually seen in pairs, grazing along the reefs.

- **The jacks** are a strong fast moving family, carnivorous and silver in colour. They are sleek, and have scimitar-like tails. Their many species include the great amberjack, crevalle jack, pompano, palometa and the permit. These fish are usually seen in transit from one point to another although the barjack is a common reef dweller. This fish has a brilliant blue band along the hind part of its back and moves with ease and grace as it seeks the small fish which are its prey.

Fig 6.47 The black stripe running through the eye of these banded butterflyfish, *Chaetodon striatus*, may act as disruptive camouflage confusing predators who cannot tell which end is the front!

Fig 6.48 Jacks are mid-water predators – fast, sleek and active. These are horse-eye jacks, *Caranx latus*.

Fig 6.49 The hog snapper, *Lachnolaimus maximus*, is not a snapper but a large wrasse. This one is eating a bivalve mollusc.

- **The wrasses** are a truly large family of fish found on the Caribbean reefs and perhaps the most diversified of all fish families in body form and size. The largest is the so-called hog 'snapper'. However, most wrasses are small, swarming about on the shallower reefs. They feed upon invertebrates and are diurnal. At night many smaller species bury themselves in the sand. They are usually brightly and often gaudily coloured.

- **The porcupines** are known for their ability to expand to several times their normal size when pursued. The body is covered with spines that protrude when the fish swells, thus discouraging a predator. The fish has a large, powerful, beak-like jaw to crush hard-shelled invertebrates upon which it feeds.

Fig 6.50 Porcupine fish, *Diodon hystrix*, can inflate themselves for protection. Here is the predator's view of such a fish – not an easy mouthful.

Fig 6.51 The peacock flounder, *Bothus lunatus*, is a typical flatfish which spends much of its time half hidden on sandy seabeds.

- **The flounders**, or flatfishes, are distinctive in that both eyes are on one side. In the larval stage the eyes are in a normal position, until one begins to migrate to the opposite side of the head. A colourful species is the peacock flounder, which is hard to find when resting on the sandy bottom but as soon as it starts to cruise over the sand distinct blue markings appear.

MISUNDERSTOOD 'MONSTERS' OF THE SEA

It is regrettable that legends, fictional stories and movies have caused man to fear some of the sea's most harmless creatures. Even when there is cause for caution the risks are often exaggerated.

- **The stingrays** are very primitive fish with cartilaginous skeletons. They are related to the sharks but have become adapted to life on the seabed as can be seen from their flattened form. They usually lie on the bottom, partially buried in the sand, and feed by excavating shallow depressions to expose invertebrates. Many rays bear live young. The majestic spotted eagle rays attain a width of over 6 feet (2 m). They glide singly or in small groups over shallow sand flats or deep reefs. Very shy, rays will usually flee from any diver; if stepped on, however, a ray will use his sharp barb, at the base of the tail, for defence. If stingrays are approached from the side or the front they can raise their sting making thrusting movements. Approached from behind they are unable to fence in this way and are relatively innocuous.

Fig 6.52 Like the flounders, stingrays are bottom dwellers. This is the southern stingray, *Dasyatis americana*.

Fig 6.53 The rays also include the spotted eagle ray, *Aetobatus narinari*, which may reach a 'wingspan' of 7 feet (over 2 m).

- **The sharks**, relatives of the rays, are abundant in all seas, and are perhaps most feared by man. Some are harmless; others are not. Their primitive nature and reputation as voracious scavengers make divers cautious in their presence. Close to shore sharks are seldom seen but an occasional nurse shark may be encountered sleeping on the bottom. It feeds on small invertebrates and is shy by nature, but still capable of biting! More dangerous are the tiger and reef sharks. Both feed mainly on fish and turtles but have been known to be aggressive. Some attacks on humans by tiger sharks have been fatal. Hammerhead sharks are also regarded as dangerous although in some places resident hammerheads have peacefully shared space with divers over long periods. Most shark attacks have been associated with humans involved in fishing, either carrying spearfishing catches or even standing in shallow water cleaning the catch. It would seem that the 'smell' of the fish has been the initial attraction but clearly sharks should be regarded with respect at all times. Having said that, the safest shark to approach may be the biggest! The world's biggest fish is the whale shark reaching 65 feet (20 m) in length but it feeds on small fish and invertebrate plankton. You may be just lucky enough to see one cruising in deep water but they are very rare.

Fig 6.54 The commonest of the reef dwelling sharks is the mild-mannered nurse shark, *Ginglymostoma cirratum*. This specimen has a remora attached to its pectoral fin.

- **The eels** occupy their coral caves or remain buried in the bottom sediment by day and search for food at night. Normally shy, eels have been known to attack spearfishermen carrying dead or dying fish. Local species include the congers, snake eels and morays. The green moray can attain a length of over 6 feet (2 m).

- **The great barracuda** has a nasty sneer which is enough to frighten any diver; however, these fish are more curious than aggressive, and habitually follow divers at fixed distances. Almost all recorded attacks on people have occurred in murky water where the barracuda could have easily mistaken the bather's limbs for a flailing fish. Under such conditions the bites have usually been directed at bright metallic objects such as

Fig 6.55 The spotted moray, *Gymnothorax moringa*, is a frightening site as it eyes you up from its refuge.

Fig 6.56 We are always being reassured that the great barracuda, *Sphyraena barracuda*, is usually harmless. However, they still have the ability to inspire fear perhaps because of their scowling eyes and massive jaws.

divers' watches or gauges which presumably flash like the silvery scales of the normal prey. Barracudas can reach over 6 feet in length, but most inhabiting local waters are under 5 feet (1.5 m).

- **The octopus**, a highly intelligent mollusc, attains a length of only about 16 inches (40 cm) in the Caribbean. By day it hides in a hole on the bottom, discernible by a pile of empty shells at the entrance, leftovers from its meals. It can change colour rapidly to blend with the surroundings, as can its relative the squid, also found in local waters and growing no larger than about 12 inches (30 cm). As a defence mechanism, both creatures emit clouds of black ink when frightened. In the case of squid, which are mid-water swimming creatures, the release of ink is very fast. The ink ejected makes a black 'blob' in the water about the same size as the squid which, at the same time, performs a very rapid backward movement. The observer's eye is held by the ink patch and misses the now-departed squid. A further elaboration of this complex escape mechanism is that the previously dark squid changes colour as it moves to become pale and almost invisible.

In general, the so-called 'monsters' of the sea are harmless if left alone. Most are scavengers, feeding upon dead or sick creatures, cleaning up Nature's 'garbage'. Those of us who venture beneath the sea must respect the territorial rights of all creatures found there, for it is their world, and Man is only an uninvited guest.

MECHANISMS FOR OFFENCE AND DEFENCE

It has been mentioned that fish school for protection, for there is indeed safety in numbers. Some fish, however, use rather artful forms of camouflage, both to capture and to hide from other creatures. An example is the long and slender trumpetfish. It may hang vertically in the water next to a tall coral branch, attempting to disguise itself. Occasionally the clever trumpet may travel with a school of tangs, appearing appropriately blue, to blend with its companions. At other times the trumpets are seen literally riding the backs of groupers in an attempt to be 'invisible'.

Some fish are endowed by Nature with disruptive coloration, intricate markings on the body of the fish that confuse a predator. The four-eyed butterflyfish, for instance, has a large black spot at

Fig 6.57 The four-eyed butterflyfish, *Chaetodon capistratus*, is so-called because the black spot near the tail looks like an extra eye. Presumably predators are confused too.

Fig 6.58 The spotted scorpionfish, *Scorpaena plumieri*, is well camouflaged which is unfortunate for unwary divers or swimmers as it also has toxin-filled spines on its dorsal fins. A misplaced foot or hand can result in a very painful sting that may well need medical attention.

the base of its tail. Resembling an eye, it fools the pursuer into miscalculating the direction of the chase. Fish may also contain toxins in their flesh or exude poisonous mucus, as is the case with the trunkfishes. It is presumed that these poisons are defensive. Poisonous or harmful animals often advertise their presence with bright colours (e.g. yellow and black wasps, coral snakes and many distasteful insects). However, this does not often seem to be the case with fish, perhaps because many quite harmless fish are brightly coloured for other reasons. Indeed some of the most hazardous fishes in the Caribbean, the scorpionfish, are very well camouflaged (although it must be admitted that some Indo-Pacific species are brightly coloured). These fish, sometimes called stonefish, are aptly named for they do indeed look like stones lying on the seabed or on a coral reef and they do have a sting like a scorpion. The poison is contained in sacs at the base of the dorsal fin spines. An unwary predator or human will find these poison barbs very unpleasant indeed.

The toxic fish mentioned above produce their own poison. However, occasionally, fish of various types can cause poisoning when eaten. These are usually predatory reef fish (e.g. barracuda) and the poison they contain has been passed to them from the fish upon which they feed. These in turn have received the toxin from their food and so on. The original source of the poison is in an alga. Research is being carried out to devise a simple test to detect the poison in affected fish.

FISH COLOURS AND TERRITORIES

Why is it that many reef fish are so colourful? There may be different answers and certainly there is no one reason which applies to all the colourful species. However, many are undoubtedly advertising their presence to other members of the same species. Such fish live relatively solitary lives, not forming schools but staying put on one small piece of reef. If another member of its own species wanders by it will be chased out of the area which the owner fish regards as its territory. Usually these encounters do not result in injury because the intruder seems to accept its misbehaviour and loses no time in rushing away. If, however, the intruder cannot easily escape then fights will result which can, and do, result in the death of one or other of the combatants. It is for this reason that only one individual of such species can be kept in a small aquarium tank. Sometimes other species will be attacked if they have either similar colours or a similar shape.

Territorial behaviour is commonly found in a wide variety of animals including birds and mammals. The territory may be held for a variety of reasons: to preserve a large enough area for feeding; to protect a breeding site; or to attract females. In such circumstances the territory holders will inevitably spend much time fighting off intruders and bright colours help to avoid prolonged intrusion deep into territories as would be the case if the animals were unobtrusively coloured. These bright colours carry some disadvantages however, for they render their carriers obvious to predators and one often finds that such fish are adapted for retreating into holes or crevices in the coral in the event of a predator appearing. Another problem is that if the bright colours of one's relatives provoke aggression how can mating take place? This is solved in a variety of ways. Often, for example, the adults are not so brilliantly coloured, and not so provocative to one another. A good example is the French angelfish which is striped black and gold in the juvenile but dark greyish in adulthood. The yellow-tailed damsel fish when young is bright blue and covered with lighter iridescent blue spots but in the adult form is much less striking. Some normally bright fishes take on much less bright colours

Fig 6.59 The proportion of black colour increases as the rock beauty, *Holacanthus tricolor*, grows. It is generally thought that this diminution of brightness with age may be to reduce provocation between adults and perhaps to aid predator avoidance.

when mating. The yellow, black and silver striped sergeant majors become a nearly uniform dark blue when guarding the eggs. Other brightly coloured fish lose their colours when asleep.

One species of fish, the wrasse blenny, looks very like the juvenile stages of the bluehead wrasse. The bluehead is a 'cleaner' fish and is therefore not taken by predators. Because of its resemblance, the blenny seems to be able to go abroad on the reef to get its food, small fish and crustaceans, without being attacked by larger fish. This mimicry goes beyond coloration and body shape even to an imitation of the bluehead's way of swimming.

FISH AND THE REEF

Fish on the reef have an almost infinite variety of lifestyles. Between them they are able to consume almost any plant or animal material available. Only a select few animals are immune from attack by fish. Most of these are either distasteful or perhaps well protected like the spiny black sea urchin, *Diadema*, that is so common on the reef. Its very commonness is a testament to its ability to avoid predation. There is no doubt that it makes good eating once the predator can get past the spines, for if one is broken open clouds of fish, especially the small wrasse known as slippery dicks, swim around to pick the flesh from inside the shell.

Many fish are predators on other fish. The barracuda relies on its speed over short distance to catch its prey while others lie disguised against their background waiting for unwary passers-by. The scorpionfish fall into this group, as does the curious batfish. These latter have a small fleshy protuberance sticking out from the front of their heads. By gently jiggling this they attract small fish within reach of their capacious jaws. Batfish, when young, are also said to have an uncommon resemblance to fallen mangrove leaves as they lie on the seabed. Perhaps this disguise protects them from predators as well as hiding them from their own prey. As has been mentioned, trumpetfish make themselves unobtrusive by colour change and by skilfully placing themselves near long slender objects.

Parrotfish are grazers. If they can get it they will eat algae or seagrass but often these are unavailable and the parrotfish will use its powerful jaws to rasp the surface off living coral heads. They favour the large smooth colonies of corals such as *Siderastrea*. It is not uncommon when snorkelling or diving to see the marks left by their jaws on the surface of the coral and perhaps to hear them rasping away at their work. The fish obviously remove quite large quantities of coral skeleton with the nutritious part of their meal and thus their faeces contain much fine ground coral sand. This sand settles into the spaces in the reef where eventually it is consolidated. This activity of the parrotfish is of considerable importance in reef building.

Many fish live on crustacea and molluscs in the sand near to reefs. Among these are the goatfishes which can be seen in schools moving across the seabed periodically pushing their heads into the sand and alternately sucking and blowing water through their mouths. This action throws up the sand and creates a shallow hole. In this hole the goatfish searches for food with the long barbels which are thrust down from its lower jaw. The shape of fish may open up certain areas for exploitation. For example, the handsome gold-spotted eel can slither its snake-like body into all sorts of crevices and burrows in the search for food.

Many reef fish are far more active at night than during the day. This makes a night-time dive or snorkelling trip with an underwater torch particularly interesting. Among these nocturnal fish are the squirrelfish, the voracious moray and, unfortunately, many

Fig 6.60 Lizardfish, *Synodus intermedius*, have a sinister look which is fully deserved – at least if you are a fish. These predators are capable of catching and eating fish almost as large as themselves.

species of shark. To guard against being snapped up in their sleep by these night-time prowlers many fish hide away in crevices and bury themselves in the sand (e.g. the wrasses). Some parrotfish secrete a layer of mucus around themselves while they sleep which presumably discourages would-be predators.

FISH WATCHING

Fish are undoubtedly one of the glories of coral reefs. The variety of colour, shape and movement is staggering and to SCUBA dive over or in such reefs is like swimming inside an aquarium. But does one need to go to the lengths and expense of aqua-lung diving to enjoy these sights? The answer is clearly 'no'; there are many ways in which one can observe beautiful fish. The simplest is to go to the fish wharves and markets where the fish, sometimes still alive, can be easily examined and one can learn much about their habits and so on from the fishermen too. The major problem is that these are literally fish out of water and after death their movements, and often their colours, are lost.

Why can one not walk out and watch the fish through the surface of the water? In some places one can, but even the slightest breeze or wave will disturb the surface making a clear view impossible. However, this can be counteracted by using a glass-bottomed viewing box. This can be simply made, being a wooden or metal box about 12 inches (30 cm) square and perhaps 16–20 inches (40 or 50 cm) deep. One end is open and the other is covered with a piece of fairly thick glass and the whole made watertight with putty. The observer holds the box in the water so that the glass bottom is below the surface and looks through this glass window from the top of the box. The same principle is employed in the glass-bottomed boats so common in tourist-developed areas. Here the window is somewhat bigger and is built into the bottom of a boat which can be motored out over the reef while its occupants get an excellent view of the seabed. In clear waters it is not unusual to be able to see the bottom in 100 feet (30 m) of water from such a boat.

For the swimmer a mask and snorkel have the visibility of a glass-bottomed box but with added freedom of movement. The snorkeller may prefer to float at the surface but if he takes to diving down he will be able to see the fish from the side as other fish see them and not just their backs from above. Experienced

Fig 6.61 SCUBA divers certainly do have the chance to get close to their subjects – in this case the grouper seems to be so interested in the diver that he cannot even get it in the frame.

snorkellers can dive to considerable depths – 50 feet (15 m) or more is not uncommon – but the beginner will probably be contented with dives of 7 to 10 feet (2 or 3 m).

SCUBA diving gives one almost complete freedom under water. One is no longer limited to a single breath nor to shallower depths. However, it must be remembered that this type of diving has many potential dangers and properly supervised training is essential.

Many countries in the region are also developing public aquariums where visitors and residents alike can go and study the local marine creatures under dry and convenient conditions.

A number of excellent publications exist to help the watcher identify the fish, some of these are listed in the Bibliography at the end of this book.

REEF TOGETHERNESS

A coral reef is a crowded community where diverse creatures live 'elbow to elbow'. While many organisms are continuously preying

Fig 6.62 This squirrelfish has an ectoparasitic crustacean (isopod) on its head between the eyes.

upon others for food, there exist several relationships, pairings of different species, for the benefit of one or of both. These are closer and often more than specific prey/predator relationships. Four types will be mentioned:

- **Parasitism** occurs when one organism lives in or on the body of another, obtaining nourishment at the host's expense. An example found on coral reefs is that of the soldierfish and a small crustacean, called an isopod, which fastens to the fish's forehead. Butterflyfish and grunts may also be seen to 'wear' isopods between or below their eyes. Because they cannot reach their bodies with their mouths and lack limbs for scratching, fish are plagued with these so-called ectoparasites, many of which are too tiny to be seen but nevertheless cling stubbornly to the helpless fish.

- **Commensalism**, meaning common table, is an association in which the benefit may be one-sided, although unlike parasitism the other animal appears unaffected either way. For example, one not infrequently finds polychaete worms living with hermit crabs in their shells. When the hermit crab is eating, the worm will appear and scavenge discarded food. This relationship clearly benefits the worm which gains protection and free food while apparently doing his host no harm. Likewise, there is a small fish which lives in the rectum of large sea cucumbers. It uses its strange home for protection, emerging to feed and on returning re-enters tail first. The sea cucumber is apparently unharmed by this strange visitor. However, the line between commensalism and parasitism is a very finely drawn one. This is the case with the brittlestar, *Ophiothrix*, which lives attached to sponges and soft corals holding out its arms to filter the water. It is possible, perhaps, that the brittlestar is depriving its host of food by getting first bite. The balance of benefit and harm is sometimes difficult to ascertain. For example, there is the tiny pea crab that lives inside the mussel *Brachidontes*. In this case there is clear evidence that the mussel's gills are damaged by the crab. However, the same relationship exists with the European mussel and in this case it is difficult to show any deleterious effect.

- **Mutualism** is an association which benefits both parties and to some extent offsets the one-sided parasitic relationship. Fish

Fig 6.63 This green moray, *Gymnothorax funebris*, is being cleaned of ectoparasites by a cleaner fish.

Fig 6.64 The shrimp, *Periclimenes yucatanicu*, lives in the tentacles of the anemone, immune to stinging cells and protected from predators. This shrimp will clean passing fish of their parasites. Its bright colours are probably an advertisement of its cleaner role.

with small body parasites visit cleaning stations throughout the reef. Waiting there are tiny cleaners, which may be fish or shrimp, which spend their day picking the parasites from the bodies of the patient and grateful clients. In some cases the cleaners will venture into the mouth or gill cavities of their customers. Most cleaners advertise their presence by their coloration and/or particular dance they do. Shrimp, for example, wave their long antennae frantically when a large fish comes near, broadcasting the fact that they are cleaners. In one scientific experiment, cleaners were removed from a small patch reef; soon the larger fish, overburdened by parasites, sickened and died. There is a beautiful example of an animal which has a commensal relationship with one creature and a mutualist relationship with another. This is the tiny shrimp *Pereclimenes*, a particular species of which teams up with an anemone, and has a perfect refuge within the stinging tentacles, being obviously immune to them. This shrimp cleans fish as well, emerging from its tentacled refuge to pick parasites from passing clients.

- **Symbiotic** relationships are really specialized forms of mutualism in that they favour both partners, but they are often so close and intimate that the pair become interdependent and cannot readily survive in isolation. The coral itself is the best example here, for as has been explained, many of the coral polyp cells contain unicellular algae, each contributing to the other's well being. Many other cases of symbiosis are known often involving organisms from very different groups. Some hydroids or sea anemones will attach themselves to the shells of hermit crabs while other crabs have sponges growing on their shells. The advantage to the crabs lies in protection or camouflage while the advantage to the sessile creatures is that of locomotion. Another marine example is that of the yellowish lichens that can be seen on some rock surfaces in the splash zone. These, like all other lichens, are composite creatures containing both an alga and a fungus. So intimate is this relationship that the resultant plant can in many ways be deemed to be new and independent; more than simply the sum of its parts.

The presence of so many examples of mutualism and symbiosis in the coral reef is one indication of the extreme closeness of the community and, through the retention and efficient transfer of nutrients, one of the factors which leads to its success.

THE CORAL ECOSYSTEM

A living coral reef is a community composed of thousands of different members living in harmony with one another. The existence of the reef is based upon physical, biological and chemical interactions among all its inhabitants. This interdependence is so vital that many of the reef dwellers cannot live outside the reef zone. Sunlight, water, fish and lower animals play their role in building and sustaining the coral reef. Sunlight fosters photosynthesis necessary to the tiny single-celled plants that live in the coral tissues. Water brings nutrients to the entire community. The lower animals secrete hard calcium carbonate that cements the community together, and the excrement of fish and other animals helps to build up the reefs.

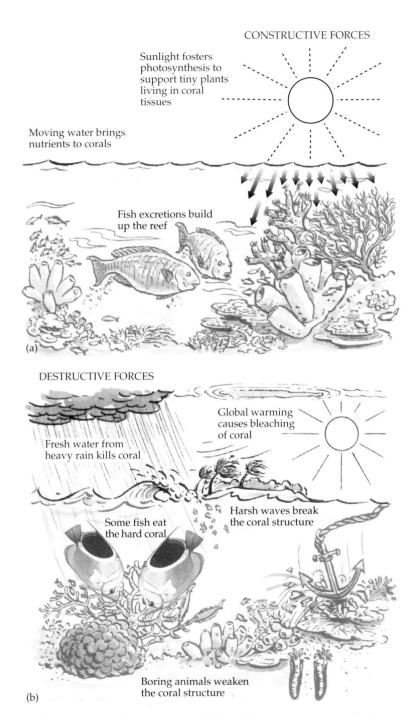

CONSTRUCTIVE FORCES

Sunlight fosters photosynthesis to support tiny plants living in coral tissues

Moving water brings nutrients to corals

Fish excretions build up the reef

(a)

DESTRUCTIVE FORCES

Global warming causes bleaching of coral

Fresh water from heavy rain kills coral

Some fish eat the hard coral

Harsh waves break the coral structure

Boring animals weaken the coral structure

(b)

Fig 6.65a, b The coral ecosystem. (a) Constructive forces. (b) Destructive forces.

7 The Open Sea

PLANKTON

Most of the Caribbean region is covered by water. Around the islands, and in the areas north of Antigua and around the Bahamas, the sea is shallow. In these shallow places the marine life is considerably affected by the underlying seabed which is usually rich in corals. In reality these areas constitute a vast coral reef.

However, over the rest of the Caribbean the sea is deep, typically over 6500 feet (2000 m) and as much as 22,750 feet (7000 m) in the Cayman Trench. Life in these deep waters is essentially a floating one. It requires energy which is supplied by the sun in the form of light and is captured by the plants and converted into chemical energy by the process of photosynthesis. Photosynthesis is mainly carried out by microscopic floating plants which together form the phytoplankton. This provides, either directly or indirectly, the source of energy for the other creatures living in the sea. In tropical seas the population of phytoplankton is often sparse due to low levels of essential nutrients, especially nitrate, phosphate and iron. In contrast to this, phytoplankton in some places can be so plentiful as to colour the sea, being responsible for the so-called 'red tides'. Far from being coloured by the plants the Caribbean owes its wonderful clarity to their scarcity. As the plants rely on sunlight for their energy, and hence their growth and reproduction, they can only flourish in the upper layers of the sea into which the light can penetrate. Light penetrates to different depths depending on the time of day and year, and on the sky and sea conditions. In the Caribbean photosynthesis does not take place below about 200 feet (60 m) and most takes place in the top 30 feet.

Phytoplankton organisms can be very small indeed, about one two-thousandths of an inch (less than one-hundredth of a millimetre) very often. Some are larger and may be anything up two-hundredths of an inch (about one-tenth of a millimetre). To help prevent them from sinking into the dark zone of the sea these tiny plants are often equipped with hair-like flagella with which they can swim, or lighter-than-water oil droplets that buoy them up. Others slow down their sinking by having spikes or spines that act in a similar way to a parachute.

The tiny plants of the phytoplankton are eaten by herbivorous animals, many of them also small. These animals make up the zooplankton and belong to a wide variety of animal groups. The commonest are the crustacea, relatives or immature stages of the better-known crabs and lobsters. Usually they are barely visible to the naked eye (about one-fiftieth of an inch or half a millimetre). Some may pass their whole life in the plankton while others are young or larval stages of animals which, when adult, live elsewhere. Many bottom-living crabs, molluscs, worms and echinoderms start their lives by spending weeks or months drifting in the upper layers of the sea. The small larvae are able to exploit the tiny phytoplankton plants until they are large enough to cope with bigger food. The swimming and floating youngsters also help to distribute their kind over a large area, a fact of particular importance to sedentary or attached species. It is known, for example, that the larvae of the pen shell, *Pinna*, can drift the full width of the Atlantic to settle on the east coast of the USA having been spawned on the coasts of Africa.

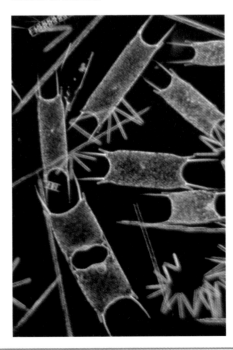

Fig 7.1 These strange organisms are mostly single-celled plants which come from the floating community of phytoplankton. Phytoplankton occurs in all of the world's seas and oceans and although there are differences between the species found in tropical and temperate seas, their role is the same, namely to be the major photosynthesisers. Typically these plants measure only thousandths of an inch (0.1 mm) or less.

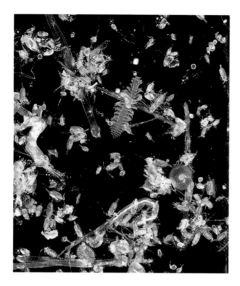

Fig 7.2 In contrast to Fig 7.1, the creatures seen here are the animals of the plankton, known as zooplankton. Most are crustaceans but many other groups are represented – from worms to larval fish. Most are just hundredths of an inch (approx. 1 mm) or so in length but some zooplankton organisms may be quite large such as the krill on which the baleen whales feed.

Larger animals may also live out their lives in the deep seas, some in the illuminated upper layers, some in the dark abyssal depths. In the surface regions many of these animals are filter feeders sieving out the plant and animal plankton. The largest animal

Fig 7.3 Juvenile fish sometimes school near the surface in deep water.

in the world, the blue whale, is one such, straining thousands of gallons of seawater each day to extract its crustacean food. Most, however, are much smaller and include the larvaceans, floating relatives of the sea-squirts. Others catch their prey with stinging tentacles. One of these is the beautiful but unpleasant Portuguese man-o'-war, *Physalia*, a relative of the jellyfish and sea anemones. This animal has a gas-filled bladder which floats at the surface of the sea. It is coloured brilliant blue or violet and may be 6 inches (15 cm) in length. From the bladder, tentacles several feet long trail down into the sea armed with powerful stinging cells. Large specimens catch and eat quite big fish. When floating near beaches or washed up on the sand they are a considerable hazard to bathers and should be avoided if at all possible. The sting is very painful at best and, at worst, a danger to life.

Floating snails are also attractive creatures and altogether safer to handle. There are two main groups, one which swims by means of an enlarged foot and the other which hangs in a floating mass of mucus and air bubbles. *Janthina* is an example of such a pelagic snail; its beautiful violet and purple shell is occasionally washed up on beaches.

There is only one large oceanic plant of any importance – the sargassum weed. This floating seaweed is a member of the genus *Sargassum*, many species of which are normally attached forms found on rocky shores. The floating forms are capable of completing their whole life cycle far from land. This seaweed is common in the Caribbean and has an associated fauna of animals adapted for

Fig 7.4 Sargassum weed, *Sargassum* spp., can grow attached to rocky shores but it is equally at home floating free in the open sea. In these conditions it frequently has its own associated fauna including the bizarre sargassum fish, *Histro histro*.

life in its forest. These include bryozoans, small colonial creatures, the crab *Portunus sayi* and a number of fishes. Most of the inhabitants are camouflaged which makes them difficult to detect. The sargassum fish in particular have taken the form and colour of the weed and are very bizarre creatures. The inhabitants of the weed are not typical pelagic animals but rather they are related to the inshore animals from which they have evolved.

The animals that live deep in the dark regions depend, either directly or indirectly, on the animal and plant material that 'falls' from the productive layers above. Some of course survive by eating their fellows, whom they often lure with a luminescent 'bait' which they dangle just in front of their mouths like the weird batfish. Although much of what falls from above is snapped up, a small amount settles on the seabed where it is eaten by bottom dwellers (including many brittlestars and bivalves) or broken down by bacteria. Needless to say the quantity of food that gets down that far is small and this, combined with very low temperatures, means that growth is slow. The hard shells of planktonic organisms are not all recycled and may accumulate on the sea floor to enormous depths, perhaps hundreds of feet thick. Many present-day limestones, chalks and siliceous earths are the result of such accumulations from the past.

FISH

At the very top of the food chain of deep-sea herbivores and carnivores come the large pelagic fish. These powerful, streamlined fish are almost always good eating and this, combined with their violent activity when hooked, has made them favourites with professional and sport fishermen alike. The encounter between man and these huge fish has been immortalized in Hemingway's *The Old Man and the Sea*: 'Never have I seen a greater, or more beautiful, or a calmer or more noble thing than you, brother', says Hemingway's hero of a huge marlin probably weighing nearly half a ton.

Commercial fishermen are usually less ambitious about their fish and a 22 pound (10 kg) kingfish or dolphin, as well as smaller tuna and albacore, are more typical catches. These are most often caught on lines trailed behind the boat, but are sometimes netted. Netting is usually carried out by very large fishing boats which may travel many thousands of miles to find good fishing grounds.

Fig 7.5 Much of the local fishing is done from small boats. These often have a distinct regional appearance, like these characteristic Jamaican craft.

- **Marlin** are all fast swimming predators and include some of the most famous sport fish. Many of them have the bones of the upper jaw extended into a long, pointed rostrum. It is said that this 'sword' is used to club smaller fish. There are also numerous records of ships and boats being attacked by swordfish. The penetrative power of the sword would be hard to believe if it were not for many examples of fish breaking them off and leaving them embedded in the boat's woodwork. The British Museum has such a sword that had penetrated 21 inches (55 cm) of planking before snapping.

- **Tuna** are not usually as large as the marlin and often hunt in schools. Fishermen who can locate these schools sometimes catch hundreds of pounds of fish in a few minutes, as they will take baited hooks with no hesitation. They are very fast swimmers and, although authenticated reports are difficult to obtain, speeds of up to 35 mph (55 kmph) are probably not an underestimate. Three factors contribute to their speed. Firstly, they are beautifully streamlined, fitting almost exactly the engineer's specifications for maximum hydrodynamic efficiency. Secondly, their tails are strengthened by the continuation of the backbone into it, unlike other fish whose tails contain only small bony rays for support. As a result the tail of the tuna is remarkably stiff

Fig 7.6 These tarpon, *Megalops atlanticus*, make for a big catch. This fish is a large relative of the temperate water herring.

and strong. Thirdly, many tuna have been shown to have a body temperature higher than the surrounding sea by as much as 4–5°C thus making them warm-blooded to some extent. This raised temperature enables them to work faster than their cold-blooded relatives.

- **Dolphin** is the name given to a much-prized fish in parts of the Caribbean. Needless to say the name often misleads visitors who are used to applying it to small mammals related to the whales. These latter are of course warm-blooded and suckle their young in the typical mammalian way while the creature referred to here is very much a fish. The name may have been used because of the high crest of bone on the head which gives the creature a superficial resemblance to the small whales. It is a long, rather narrow fish which may be nearly 6 feet (2 m) in length and weigh 44 pounds (20 kg) or more, although smaller specimens are more usually seen in the fish markets. In life it is brilliantly coloured, bluish above and yellow beneath but these colours quickly fade after death.

Fig 7.7 Fisheries in the region are very diverse ranging from simple, one-man operations up to representatives of the international fleets. Sadly it is now a rare sight to see these larger hand-crafted wooden boats being built on Caribbean beaches.

- **Flying fish** are common in all tropical seas but unlike the species mentioned previously they are relatively small, rarely exceeding 18 inches (45 cm) in length. The Caribbean species is about 10 inches (25 cm) long and has rather the same shape and colour as a herring. Of course the most remarkable thing about these fish is their ability to 'fly'. For many years there was debate as to whether the fish actively fly or just glide, but high-speed cinefilms have now shown that they only perform the latter. Just prior to take-off the fish swims rapidly towards the surface. It bursts out into the air at a velocity of something like 35 mph (55 kmph) and once it is airborne it spreads out its large winglike pectoral fins. Some species, including the common Caribbean one, also extend their pelvic fins and so appear to have four wings. The fish then skims over the surface of the sea, usually for a few seconds although flights of up to 15 seconds have been recorded. The distance travelled may be as much as 1250 feet (350 m) but is most often just 100–130 feet (30–40 m). This ability to 'fly' must help the fish escape from their predators, though there is some evidence that they do it just for 'fun'.

Although these fish are fairly common in the Caribbean they are only fished in any numbers from Barbados and Grenada. The season extends roughly through the first half of the year and the method of catching them is interesting. They are mainly caught at the time of spawning when the females are searching for floating objects on which to lay their sticky eggs. The fishermen go out in their boats and throw palm fronds and other debris into the sea which, together with a small basket of rotting fish held over the side, attracts the flying fish. They can then be caught in small dip nets and lifted into the boat. In recent years these traditional methods have to some extent been replaced by the use of gill nets.

- **Sharks.** No section on deep-sea fish is complete without mention of these notorious creatures. They have such a reputation and

Fig 7.8 Most of the fish caught by local fishermen are quickly sold at small markets or even from the boats at the harbour. This scene is at a cooperative market in Belize.

are surrounded by so much mythology that it is difficult to arrive at a balanced view about them. There can be no doubt that most species of shark are voracious predators and some may make unprovoked attacks on swimmers and divers. It is possible that at least some shark attacks are in defence of territory rather than as a feeding response but this has not been clearly established. Luckily the Caribbean does not suffer from shark incidents to the same extent as the Pacific. The number of authenticated attacks is small but nevertheless the sharks are there and should be treated with respect.

The deep-sea sharks which are potentially the most dangerous are those that feed on large, active prey and include the mako, tiger and hammerhead. However, even the usually placid nurse sharks have been known to bite if annoyed. Spear fishers are well advised to trail their catch on a long line well away from their bodies or to place it in a boat immediately after capture for sharks are very sensitive to both the movements of injured fish and the smell of blood.

Sharks are caught and eaten throughout the Caribbean but the quality of the meat varies a great deal from species to species.

Fig 7.9 A Caribbean reef shark. Shark attacks on humans are thankfully uncommon in the Caribbean. None the less they should always be treated with respect and caution.

8 Turtles, Birds and Marine Mammals

Most of the previous chapters have dealt with particular habitats and the plants and animals that live in them. However, when dealing with larger animals this approach sometimes breaks down as their mobility permits them to range more widely. This chapter deals with the biology of some of these larger, very mobile animals.

TURTLES

Sea turtles feed around coasts and nest on beaches throughout the tropical seas of the world. They were once abundant, but their populations have been so reduced by indiscriminate hunting that strict conservation measures are required to save them from further depletion, perhaps even extinction.

Fig 8.1 The green turtle, *Chelonia mydas*, often grazes on seagrass, hence its alternative name of turtle-grass.

Of the five species known in the Caribbean region, the **green turtle**, *Chelonia mydas*, is the most important economically. It is noted for its navigational ability, making migrations as far as 750 miles (1200 km) through open ocean to find the proper nesting area. The female green turtle lays her eggs above the high tide mark on carefully selected beaches. Approximately 100 eggs are laid at each nesting, with the female laying in an average of five nests each season at intervals of 10–15 days. The females do not lay each year, however, but in cycles of 2, 3 or 4 years.

Once a nesting beach has been selected, the nesting process passes through a number of clearly defined stages during which the adult female may be on the beach for 1 or 2 hours. On arriving at the beach, the turtle crawls a little way up from the surf line and pushes her nose into the sand. This 'sand smelling' is repeated several times until the turtle is satisfied that a suitable beach sand is present, then she crawls up the remaining portion of the beach slope, pulling with her long front flippers and pushing with the shorter rear ones. On the flatter beach crest, where the sand is dry, she may wander around for quite a while until she selects the exact spot where nesting will take place. Digging begins in the chosen site with energetic swipes of the fore limbs and sand is thrown back over the body until a wide pit has been excavated. She settles down

Fig 8.2 Turtles lay their eggs in holes excavated on sandy shores. This female green turtle is in the process of digging a nest hole with her front flippers.

Fig 8.3 When the nest hole is completed the eggs are deposited in it. Here we can see the newly-laid eggs and the posterior tip of the turtle's carapace. After the eggs are laid the hole will be filled in so as to completely bury them.

in one part of this body pit, firmly anchored by stretching out her flippers to the side, and commences digging the nest hole. The eggs will be laid in a bottle-shaped hole about 24 to 30 inches (60–80 cm) deep which is excavated by alternate movements of the hind flippers. Each flipper digs out a small lump of sand and throws it away to one side. As the hole deepens, the sensitive tips of the flippers test the depth and carefully shape and smooth the walls until it is ready to receive the eggs. Egg laying then proceeds, the eggs falling into the nest hole two or three at a time over about half an hour. The turtle next pulls sand into the hole with the hind flippers and packs it down firmly on top of the eggs. Once they are covered and the top of the hole obliterated, she starts working again with the front flippers. These now throw sand backwards to bury the whole nest area and the turtle will move this way and that, throwing sand all the while, until it is almost impossible to detect the exact spot where nesting took place.

Her job completed, the female turtle must now return to the sea to feed until the next batch of eggs is ready for laying. During the covering up movements on the beach crest, the turtle has been reorientating herself to the sea. She has been responding to visual signals which tell her that she must move towards the brightest part of the horizon. The sky over the nearby sea is brighter than that over the land, so she moves off in this direction. Her orientation to brightness is strengthened when she begins to move downhill on reaching the beach slope, and once she feels the surf on her body new vigour seems to be gained and she swims swiftly out to sea.

A few green turtles nest on some Caribbean islands but the vast majority of those that live and feed in the region nest in one of two important rookeries. Many migrate each year to the tiny, low-lying Aves Island to lay their eggs, while hundreds of others visit the Tortuguero Beach in Costa Rica. The relative seclusion and inaccessibility of these two areas accounts for the continued presence of nesting turtles which have been destroyed in so many other parts of the Caribbean. Active conservation programmes on Aves and in Costa Rica over the past few years have contributed greatly to the hatching success of the green turtle.

The turtle eggs that have been buried in the sand hatch in about 60 days and the hatchlings work their way to the surface by struggling and digging upwards together. Emergence from the nest occurs almost always at night and the baby turtles immediately scramble for the ocean. Like their mothers they orient themselves towards the brighter horizon which indicates the direction of the sea. Any sort of artificial light on the landward side of the beach can cause disorientation in both adult and young turtles and consequently increase mortality at this vulnerable time.

Hatchlings are particularly susceptible to predation by crabs while on the beach. Even upon entering the sea, the baby turtles must still contend with sharks and other large fish as well as attacks by sea birds. Should emergence from the nest take place in daylight many of the hatchlings will be eaten by birds before they reach the sea. It is estimated that, due to predation, only one or two turtles from each batch of about 100 eggs laid survives to become sexually mature. Maturity is reached in from 4 to 6 years, when these survivors will join the other adults in their nesting migration and, thereby, complete the life cycle.

Fig 8.4 Green turtle hatchlings heading for the sea.

It is still not known where the young sea turtles spend the first year of their life, although it is assumed that they swim far out to sea and feed on small floating crustaceans and molluscs. After about one year they return to inshore waters and feed primarily in seagrass beds. An individual turtle will graze the same patch of bed producing a short turf known as a scar. In such scars the new growth of seagrass is relatively rich in nutrients. Green turtles can reach a length of over 3.25 feet (1 m) and may weigh as much as 550 pounds (250 kg).

The past four centuries have witnessed a vast decline in the number of green and, too some extent, other turtles. Early sailing ships relied heavily upon this resource to provide meat during trips across the Atlantic. With increasing world population and the resulting demand for more protein, this type of exploitation has multiplied until today there are only remnants of the previously existing turtle populations, and many former nesting beaches are no longer visited by sea turtles. There are three aspects of the life history of turtles which make them vulnerable to predation by man:

firstly, the female must leave the protection of the sea to lay her eggs; secondly, large numbers of turtles tend to lay at the same time; and thirdly, females usually return to the same beach several times during one nesting season. Man has been responsible for the reduction of sea turtle populations by killing the adults at sea and while nesting on beaches and by taking large numbers of eggs from nesting beaches for food. In addition, the development of many former nesting beaches into resort areas has driven away the turtles.

Not only are green turtle eggs and meat used for food, but also turtle soup is made from the cartilage (calipee) from under the shell. In addition, the shiny plates from the outside of the carapace or back of green and hawksbill turtles have been used for jewellery and decorative work and small, whole shells have been sold as tourist items. The skin, particularly from around the neck and shoulders, produces a good quality reptile leather. All sea turtles are now on Appendix I of the Committee on International Trade in Endangered Species of Wild Fauna and Flora (CITES) which bans all commercial international trade in turtles and turtle products. It is an offence to import such products into countries which are signatories to CITES agreements (including the USA and UK). In the past there have been turtle farms in the Caribbean, notably in the Cayman Islands. They took hatchlings into culture where they were fed until they were of a suitable size to slaughter for the various useful parts. These operations were justified, in part, by the return of some juveniles and sub-adults to the sea. It was claimed that by protecting the extremely vulnerable hatchlings through the early months of their lives, these returned animals would result in an increase in the adult population more than offsetting the reduction due to hatchling removal. This claim may be true although little or nothing is known of the fate of these returnees, naive in the ways of the wild and not previously required to fend for themselves. CITES has agreed in principle to consider permitting the renewal of trade from such ranching operations but subject to extremely rigorous regulations, which would require the host country to have a national management plan for sea turtles and for the ranching proposal to 'take the lead in the development and effective implementation of a regional management protocol designed to enhance the conservation of the population'.

Active conservation of sea turtles requires, of course, more than just CITES listing. Much has been done in the Caribbean in the last two decades through organizations such as WIDECAST. This group works hard to educate and to raise local awareness of turtles and the need for their conservation. In general there is now better protection of nest site beaches and a higher level of protection for adults both at sea and on beaches. None the less, much remains to be done.

- **The hawksbill turtle**, *Eretmochelys imbricata*, is distinguished, as its name implies, by its narrow, pointed beak. Its food preference is for sponges; a Caribbean-wide study of these turtles has shown that over 95 per cent of the gut content was sponges. These are torn off rocks and crushed by the strong hawk-like beak before being swallowed. Like the green turtle, divers often see this species as it sleeps under water in holes and crevices on rocky shores and coral reefs. This species produces the best quality turtle shell and in the past has been traded in significant quantities. Fishermen regard it as relatively easy to catch and it is still eaten in a number of places in the Caribbean. It breeds widely throughout the region. Typically, females will nest 4–6 times per year depositing over 100 eggs on each occasion.

Fig 8.5 This hawksbill turtle, *Eretmochelys imbricata*, is seen against the backdrop of a coral reef. The diet of this turtle is mainly sponges which it tears from the reef with its beak-like jaws.

Fig 8.6 Loggerhead turtles, *Caretta caretta*, are occasionally sighted in inshore waters.

- **The loggerhead turtle**, *Caretta caretta*, can be recognized by its unusually large head and thick neck. It reaches a length of about 4 feet (1.2 m) and a weight of 440 pounds (200 kg). Loggerhead backs are often covered with encrusting barnacles, which are uncommon on other species. Its heavy jaws play their part in the animal's feeding which mainly involves molluscs and hard-shelled crabs. Loggerhead shell is little used in the turtle trade, although meat and eggs are taken readily.

- **The olive ridley turtle**, *Lepidochelys olivacea*, is the smallest of the local sea turtle species and reaches only about 2 feet (0.6 m) carapace length with a weight of about 100 pounds (45 kg). It feeds largely on shellfish and other marine animals collected in coastal waters. It nests two or three times each season at beaches in the southern part of the region, notably in Surinam, Guyana and French Guiana. Nesting numbers have declined in Surinam from about 3000 nests per year in the 1960s to fewer than 500 nests per year in the 1990s.

- **Kemp's ridley turtle**, *Lepidochelys kempi*, is closely related to the olive ridley turtle but a more northerly species widespread in the Gulf of Mexico and the temperate North Atlantic. However, it nests at one site in the Caribbean, namely Rancho Nuevo in Mexico. As with the olive ridley there has been a marked decline in the numbers nesting from 42,000 females nesting in one day in 1947 to fewer than 500 nesting females per year in 1993.

Fig 8.7 Olive ridley turtles, *Lepidochelys olivacea*, are relatively small. This adult is more or less fully grown.

- **The leatherback turtle**, *Dermochelys coriacea*, is the largest of the world's sea turtles (adults may have carapace lengths of 5.4 feet (1.65 m) and weigh 1100 pounds (500 kg)). In general form they differ greatly from the other turtles considered here. As the name implies this turtle does not have a hard-shelled carapace but one which is flexible and with a leathery covering of smooth dark skin, sometimes spotted with white. It has very long fore flippers, almost equal to the length of the animal, which are clearly an adaptation to its pelagic life far out in the ocean, where it feeds on animal food, particularly jellyfish. It visits Caribbean beaches between March and September for nesting, and seems to prefer those with rough surf, coarse sand and a steep beach slope. A small number of leatherbacks nest on most West Indian islands but this species is more often seen in Trinidad, Colombia and the Guianas; very large nesting populations visiting Surinam and French Guiana each year. The nesting process is closely similar to that described for the green turtle and may occur as many as seven times each season at intervals of about 10 days. This species is the least popular with man, although in some parts of the region its eggs and meat are eaten.

Fig 8.8 In contrast to olive ridley turtles (Fig 8.7), leatherback turtles are much bigger, reaching to nearly 6.5 feet (2 m) in length and up to 1100 pounds (500 kg) in weight.

Fig 8.9 All species of turtle living in the Caribbean are to a greater or lesser extent endangered. They face a range of threats relating mainly to destruction or disturbance of their nesting beaches or to predation by man. This predation may be intentional or accidental but a dead turtle is a dead turtle whatever the motive. Organizations such as WIDECAST work hard to conserve the region's turtles through a range of methods including political pressure and education. This logger-head was ensnared in a shrimp net.

There is a tendency to neglect the importance of birds in marine and coastal environments, mainly because they usually fly away when we humans appear – a case of 'out of sight, out of mind' perhaps. Furthermore, the relatively low levels of production in tropical seas and the absence of large tidal fluctuations (which make intertidal areas available to birds for feeding) do not favour high densities of oceanic or coastal birds in the Caribbean. For the coastal areas of the mainland this situation is somewhat different with sea and shore birds being partially sustained by the mainland resources. In the islands, however, bird biodiversity is fairly low (as is usual for islands) and marine birds are no exception. The Society of Caribbean Ornithology recognizes 22 species of sea bird in the region including 6 which are endemic. Of this list 5 are critically endangered, 3 endangered, 4 vulnerable and 2 near threatened. In other words almost two-thirds of the total give cause for concern.

- **The brown pelican**, *Pelecanus occidentalis*, is a bird that is often seen from beaches. These big birds dive into the sea to capture fish. The large flap of skin which can stretch down from the

Fig 8.10 Brown pelicans, *Pelecanus occidentalis*, are frequently seen from the beach, either singly or in groups. They may be seen diving into the sea to capture the fish which constitute their diet. This adult is seen at its breeding site in mangroves.

lower mandible helps in this process, acting almost as a scoop net. Pelicans will sometimes work together to round up schools of fish into a compact group that can be more easily caught. They nest in coastal vegetation including mangroves. Sadly their nesting distribution is being restricted due to a number of influences including disturbance by man and by the nest-raiding activities of rats. As a consequence nesting now takes place mainly on smaller offshore islets. There is some concern that chemical pollution may be affecting such things as eggshell thickness in pelicans which in turn would decrease their reproductive success.

- **The laughing gull**, *Larus atricilla*, is the commonest gull in the Caribbean islands. This gull is black headed in the summer breeding season but in winter the head is mottled and thus looks grey from a distance.

Fig 8.11 The laughing gull, *Larus atricilla*, is the commonest gull to be seen from Caribbean beaches. These are in winter plumage, lacking the black head of their summer dress.

Fig 8.12 The magnificent frigate bird, *Fregata magnificens*, is most often seen gliding at some height along the line of the beach. It has a striking outline in flight with long narrow wings and a forked tail. This is a female at a roost site in mangroves; a male can be seen in Fig 9.10.

- **The magnificent frigate bird**, *Fregata magnificens*, is also often seen flying above the shoreline. Usually seen drifting along on the trade wind, the scimitar-winged, fork-tailed silhouette of this bird identifies it immediately. These birds nest in the Caribbean in similar sites to brown pelicans. During the breeding season the male has a scarlet throat pouch which can be inflated during courtship displays.

- **The cattle egret**, *Bubulcus ibis*, is a bird often seen at the coast and which seems to be increasing in numbers and range. This small white heron is to be found not only at the shore but it is also widely distributed inland. It is also often seen nesting with pelicans and frigate birds. Of course, other terrestrial species will make use of the seashore under certain circumstances. In Jamaica the local endemic species of grackle will rob holiday-makers of their picnics given half a chance.

MARINE MAMMALS

Although not often seen from beaches and only viewed at sea infrequently, no account of marine life would be complete without mentioning these charismatic and beautiful animals. Of the various groups of marine mammals, those which inhabit the Caribbean for at least part of their lives include the manatees, whales and dolphins.

- **The manatee**, *Trichechus manatus*, was once common throughout the Caribbean as witnessed by its bones being a widespread component of Arawak rubbish heaps from the first millennium AD. Sadly it is now only to be found in any number at the north and the south of the region particularly in the tidal estuaries and harbours of Florida and the waterways of Guyana. The manatee is a mild-mannered, slow-moving herbivore whose way of life has made it easy prey in the past for the indigenous of the peoples of the Caribbean. In Florida its tendency to float or swim close to the surface of the water and to be relatively unafraid of man's presence leads to frequent deaths or injury from boat

Fig 8.13 A female manatee with her calf. These slow-moving herbivores live in relatively shallow water and are susceptible to injury by passing boats.

propellers, lock gates and fishing gear. Tens of manatees are killed each year in such accidents and many bear horrifying scars of lucky escapes. In Guyana manatees have been introduced into and encouraged to live in the slow-flowing drainage canals where they help to keep down waterweeds by their grazing. This grazing of the weed probably also reduces mosquito populations as the aquatic larvae have fewer places to hide and so get eaten by fish. Over a 20-year period some 200 manatees have been introduced into the canals of Guyana, each of them eating up to 90 pounds (40 kg) of vegetation per day. These gentle giants occur in small but fairly stable numbers in the mangrove swamps, estuaries and rivers of mainland countries bordering the Caribbean but are absent from the Antillean islands.

- **Whales** Many whales have very wide distributions which include the Caribbean but only one, the humpback, is to be seen on a regular basis. The **humpback whale**, *Megaptera novaeangliae*, is a huge whale living on plankton sieved from the ocean by the baleen plates on its jaws. During much of the year it has a northerly distribution (temperate oceans have higher densities of its plankton food) but between January and March relatively large numbers congregate in the northern Caribbean to breed and give birth. At these times they can be observed either simply surfacing or performing their spectacular breaching leaps from the sea. To see 30 or 40 tons of whale hurling itself almost clear of the water and then to crash back amid clouds of spray

Fig 8.14 Humpback whale performing one of its spectacular breaching leaps out of the water. Humpbacks overwinter in the Caribbean, dispersing to temperate waters during the northern summer and autumn.

is the whalewatcher's experience of a lifetime. Those with especially good fortune have been able to swim with the whales and observe the vast bulk and grace of these immense animals whose average length is nearly 50 feet (15 m). At the end of their stay in the Caribbean the newly pregnant females and immature animals leave first while the females with newly-born calves stay longest in the warm tropical sea.

- **Dolphins**   As with whales, many species of dolphin have wide distributions that include our region. Sadly, however, although they are rather more common they are less predictable than the humpbacks. None the less both the **common dolphin**, *Delphinus delphis*, and the **spotted dolphin**, *Stella attenuata*, are seen fairly frequently either from boats and ships (where they often accompany the vessel, jumping clear of the surface alongside the bow wave) or by divers. There is considerable concern about the numbers of these highly intelligent mammals that die as a result of various types of fishing activity, in particular the many that drown in nets. The victims may well be attracted in the first place by the accumulation of fish in the nets and meet their end attempting to steal an easy meal.

Another major group of marine mammals, the pinnipeds, which include the seals and sealions, are mainly cold water species. The main Caribbean representative, the Caribbean harp seal, is extinct, having been sighted last in 1952.

Fig 8.15 Spotted dolphins swimming in shallow water. These highly vocal animals feed mainly on squid and fish.

9 Ecology and Conservation

ECOLOGY

We hear a lot today about **ecology**. What does the word mean? Essentially ecology is the study of the relationship of living things in their natural habitat. This includes both interactions between the various organisms and interactions between them and the physical world. The word comes from the Greek word *oikos* meaning home or dwelling. Thus ecology is a study which must take place in the environment. Laboratory studies and reading help but the ecologist must get out 'into the field'. Ecologists study living things in their environment in a variety of ways and with a variety of aims.

Community ecologists are interested in one particular type of habitat, or a part of it. Thus they may be interested in the way in which animals, plants and the physical environment interact in a mangrove swamp or coral reef: What eats what? Who lives where? How many of each are there? Do the numbers change during the year? What happens if there is a change in some important physical factor, e.g. water level by drainage? Clearly, the results are of vital importance to conservationists as they record how much change a community can absorb before fundamental and perhaps irreversible changes take place. They also aid in detecting alterations in the community and may enable action to be taken to prevent deleterious changes. Such studies are often called **synecology**.

Autecology is the study of one species in its habitat. Thus the autecologist may specialize in the ecology of the lobster, for example. Such a scientist will be concerned with the number of lobsters, their growth, the rate at which they produce eggs, what they eat, what eats them and so on. This work will take place in different communities as the adult lobster lives in a range of habitats while the larvae are planktonic (see page 78). Studies of this type help us to understand and possibly manage populations of various creatures. They are particularly important in the fishing industry (are the fishermen taking too many lobsters?) and in the conservation of vulnerable or endangered species.

Fig 9.1 A student at the University of the West Indies (Mona) paddles to his research site in a mangrove swamp. Only through continued research will we gain the quantity and quality of information on which to base informed decisions relating to Caribbean marine environments.

Modern ecology is particularly concerned with the two main aspects of synecology and autecology. Many synecologists are studying the way in which energy flows through a community. Virtually all of the energy in a community is derived from photosynthesis. Thus in a mangrove swamp the trees trap the sun's energy. Some of this is passed to animals that eat the trees. More of it is passed on when the leaves fall and rot on the mud. Here herbivores and detritus-eating creatures eat the leaves and their breakdown products and then they themselves are eaten by carnivores. There may be imports into, and exports from, the community; for example detritus washing in from the sea, growing fishes migrating out to the nearby reefs. Both mangrove swamps and seagrass beds are important exporters to the surrounding sea and reefs. The extent to which a community captures energy may depend on a variety of factors. For example, arctic environments may be limited by temperature. Similarly, productivity in the open tropical sea is usually very low due to the reduced level of important nutrients such as nitrate and phosphate which limit plant plankton growth. Such studies can tell us fairly precisely what a community may produce in terms of energy in a given time and so to what extent it can be cropped or exploited without detriment.

Population studies on the other hand are an offshoot of autecology and are concerned particularly with the factors that control the numbers of a given creature in the community. Generally speaking, ecologists recognize two major types of factors controlling population size, namely density-independent and density-dependent factors. The former do not depend on the size of the population. For example, a hurricane may cause widespread mortality irrespective of the density of the population while starvation, through over-exploitation of a food source, will increase with rising population density. Some forms of epidemic are worse at high population densities. Large populations will also encourage the greater increase of predators and parasites. Such studies are of importance in managing populations of commercially important species, either pests or food animals and plants. They also help us to understand some of the problems that we humans face with our rapidly rising population – problems such as the production of sufficient food, the control of disease and the management of natural resources.

Fig 9.2 The marine biology laboratory of UWI (Mona) is one of the 27 labs around the Caribbean contributing information to CARICOMP, a programme which monitors the health (or otherwise) of the major marine environments in the region (see page 156). All the region's data are processed and reviewed at the Center for Marine Sciences at UWI.

Ecologists make use of a wide variety of techniques. Their work may involve a good deal of quiet observation and recording of, say, feeding habits of reef fish. Mostly, however, they will be collecting information about the numbers and distribution of a community of animals and plants. If the community is too large to record in its entirety, small parts of it will be sampled and counted. This is most often done in one of two ways. If the habitat is likely to be changing in one direction (e.g. up the slope of a coral reef or from the seaward towards the landward side of a mangrove swamp) then a transect is appropriate. A line will be laid in some way, for instance from the water's edge to dry land in a swamp. Samples will then be collected or counted along this line or for a fixed distance either side of it. More than one such line may be used (to make the statistics more reliable) and lines may be made permanent so that counts can be repeated later to examine possible time-related effects. Alternatively, if the habitat is relatively uniform (e.g. a flat area of sandy sea floor) it may be more appropriate to sample by using quadrat squares. These are usually metal squares, which can be dropped at random on the habitat, and the organisms found inside the square counted.

It may well be necessary to capture, count and measure animals of interest. Sometimes these animals will be tagged or marked in some way so that they can be recognized in the future. Subsequent capture of tagged individuals may give information about the growth, life span and mobility of the animal. The tags will vary according to the animal, of course. Thus molluscs with hard shells (e.g. nerites) may have a small blob of paint put on them. Fish often have labels fastened through their fins while birds will have a small numbered metal ring placed round one leg. Ringed birds are often recaptured far away from their original point of ringing. By such methods we know that common terns (*Sterna hirundo*) may breed in North America, pass through the Caribbean in the autumn on their way to winter near the Antarctic before returning next spring to their breeding grounds in the North – a round trip of many thousands of miles in a single year. Crustacea (crabs, lobsters) are difficult to tag as they moult their skins when they grow. However, it is now possible to use tags which will remain with the animal even after a moult. It is important that tagged animals should not be hampered in any way by their tag as the ecologist is concerned that marked animals should in every way be regarded as normal and not subject to disadvantage because of the tag. Thus the bird ring must not be too heavy, the fish tag not likely to attract predators and the lobster tag not able to hinder moulting. In a few cases natural markings may permit recognition of individuals. The best known example of this is whales where differences in the markings on the tail flukes are unique to each individual.

Ecologists also have to obtain data on a variety of physical factors in the area of study: temperature, light levels, salinity, humidity, wind speed, rainfall and so on. Sometimes this will be done at the research site; sometimes the information can be obtained from governmental or regional institutions, e.g. weather stations.

CONSERVATION

Conservation is a very widely used but seldom defined term. Perhaps the most widely accepted definition might be 'The preservation of the environment in a pristine state or the efforts to return it to that state'. In this case 'pristine' usually means 'as it was before the impact of humans'. In a world where human impact has been going on for so long and to such profound effect this is usually unrealistic. Problems arise, also, when different individuals and groups understand the concept differently even to the point where conflict results. In the case of an area so large and so variously exploited as the Caribbean Sea, such differences of opinion and resultant conflicts are inevitable. To reconcile perfectly the needs and wishes of local populations, tourists with wide-ranging interests and the highly focused ambitions of single-interest groups (e.g. turtle or whale conservationists) is likely to be impossible. The motives of each are laudable and so in the end an integrated solution needs to be sought which gives due consideration to all those who seek to enhance, protect and sustain wildlife in the region.

Over the last three decades there have arisen a number of problems relating to Caribbean marine life – some through the direct effect of man's activity, some perhaps indirectly due to human intervention or to naturally occurring phenomena. Many of these problems are interrelated and the next few sections summarize the main issues.

◆ *The health of coral reefs*

As compared with the 1970s coral reefs, not only in the Caribbean but also worldwide, have been afflicted by a series of setbacks

Fig 9.3 Sadly, due mainly to coral diseases, spectacular heads of elkhorn coral like this one are an increasingly rare sight.

which have left them much diminished. A number of **coral diseases** have struck throughout the region. White band disease has hit the important *Acropora* species in particular. As its name implies, the disease appears as a white band of dying tissue, usually at the base of the coral, spreading upwards and leaving behind dead, bare coral skeleton. As these species are important reef builders, both in shallow water and at the seaward side of reefs, the implications for the continued growth of these reefs are huge. In many places in the Caribbean both *A. cervicornis* and *A. palmata* are almost entirely missing as living corals, although their dead skeletons still contribute to the reefs. Black band disease has affected, in particular, the massive corals such as *Montastrea annularis* and *Diploria labyrinthiformis*. Similar in its effects to white band disease but characterized by a moving zone of black slimy infection, this disease has resulted in widespread mortality. Other, perhaps less dramatic, infections have been noted such as red band and white pox diseases. The causes of these diseases are not clearly understood. Although microorganisms have been isolated from diseased tissue it is not known if these are the causative agents or simply secondary infections able to invade the coral as a result of the initial weakening. Tissue infected with black band disease contains a complex community including probably more than one species of cyanobacterium (blue-green alga). Stresses due to pollution, increased sediment load in the seawater and so on may have played a part in lowering the resistance of the corals to infection.

Coral bleaching results when the zooxanthellae are ejected from the coral tissue. This phenomenon is associated with a range of stressful circumstances such as poor water circulation, influx of fresh water or elevated temperatures. Across the globe bleaching events in corals have been observed closely correlated with 'hot spots' during the preceding warm season. These hot spots can be detected by satellite and show a sea surface temperature of 1°C or more above the long-term monthly average. The first of such bleaching events in the Caribbean was noted in 1979 but they have been repeated in a number of years subsequently. Although corals can slowly recover from bleaching, death often results. Predictions for global warming suggest that this problem will become an increasingly frequent one.

Another disease which affected corals and coral reefs indirectly was that which caused huge mortality of the **black sea urchin**,

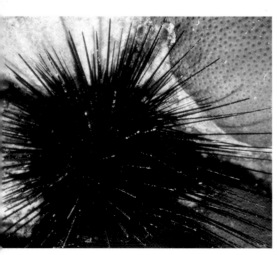

Fig 9.4 The black sea urchin, *Diadema antillarum*, is an important grazer of algae on coral reefs. Unfortunately they have been struck by disease which in the mid-1980s killed up to 95 per cent of the urchins in some locations. The release of grazing pressure resulted in increasing algal growth. Despite some recovery of urchin numbers, seaweed cover on reefs remains relatively high.

Diadema antillarum. This plague appeared first around Panama and spread rapidly throughout the region often causing the deaths of 90–95 per cent of the urchins during the mid-1980s. As the urchins feed by grazing algae on the reefs, their disappearance permitted massive increases in algal coverage on reefs already weakened by disease. This growth tends to inhibit the settlement of new corals and to be deleterious to existing corals through abrasion and overgrowth. Although there has been some recovery of urchin numbers, seaweed and other algae still cover much larger areas of reefs than formerly. In some places this problem has been made worse by overfishing of herbivorous reef fish that also play a part in keeping weed growth under control.

Added to these problems, reefs have also been adversely affected in some locations by hurricane damage, sediment deposition, organic pollution from sewage wastes and agricultural runoff.

As can be seen, coral reefs are suffering as a result of these various negative factors. Arguments rage about the extent to which human impacts are to blame for the deterioration and also about the extent to which some natural recovery and regeneration is possible. Obviously direct pollution of reefs by sewage, for example, can be controlled given the will to change the situation and the finance to arrange alternative disposal. Conservation measures such as reducing damage from anchors and from collectors have also been implemented in many places. The issues of the creation of marine parks and of overfishing are dealt with below. However,

Fig 9.5 Large seaweeds growing on the reefs constitute one of the problems that have beset coral reefs worldwide, not just in the Caribbean.

Fig 9.6 The coral reef that this parrotfish inhabits is largely dead and supporting large growths of seaweed – an all too familiar sight throughout the reefs of the world. Some of the dereliction is due to diseases and their knock-on effects but some may be due to increased sediment loads or organic pollution as a result of commercial or industrial development.

as far as disease is concerned, we simply do not know to what extent we can influence the situation either negatively or positively. Coral disease seems to have been fairly indiscriminate in striking corals in both impacted and conserved sites although there is some evidence that corals weakened by other stresses may succumb to disease more easily. Probably the situations most out of our control are those which relate to climate. Global warming seems to be producing an increasing frequency of high sea surface temperatures and thus coral bleaching. There is some suggestion, too, that hurricanes are becoming more energetic and perhaps more frequent.

◆ Fisheries

Exploitation of the fish and invertebrate populations of the Caribbean has taken place ever since Man appeared on the scene. At present the range of fishing activities is huge, varying from individual Caribbean residents fishing from the nearby shore with simple nets and traps to deep-sea fishing by vessels from the other side of the world. Between these two extremes are various types of fisheries supplying both the local and the tourist populations as well as exporting products outside the Caribbean.

Fig 9.7 A local fisherman selling his catch direct from his boat at the beach in Belize.

Deep-sea fisheries have changed over the years with different countries targeting the Caribbean: Japan, Korea, Taiwan, Venezuela and the US have all been active over the last three decades hunting a range of pelagic fish (mainly species of tuna, albacore and swordfish) using various methods (longline, purse seine, pole and line). Smaller pelagic fisheries operate from the islands and coastal countries and for them kingfish and dolphinfish are frequently favourite catches. Inshore fisheries often use homemade fish traps or small nets (including beach seines) and in some places there is little doubt that reefs are heavily overfished. It is interesting to visit local fish markets and compare the size and range of fish available with those seen while diving in conserved areas or underwater parks. Such comparisons offer convincing evidence of both overfishing and the beneficial effect of conserving stocks. There is no doubt that more controlled utilization of fish stocks would, in the long term, permit a greater total annual catch than at present. But of course such policies are unpopular to impose initially and difficult or impossible to police. As has been mentioned above, overfishing of reef fish, especially of herbivores, can lead to greater algal growth on reefs.

There are two invertebrate fisheries of considerable importance in the Caribbean, both sadly over-exploited. These are for the conch, *Strombus gigas*, and the spiny lobster, *Panulirus argus*. Both are important for export and the tourist trade. For example, in 1997 Jamaica reported export earnings of US$8–12 million from conch and US$4–6 million from lobster. Generally it is felt that both

Fig 9.8 Beach seine-netting is a popular and relatively simple means of catching fish, but this method can result in damage to the seabed if overused.

species are presently being fished at levels that cannot be sustained; indeed some experts have predicted that both these fisheries could collapse totally within the next few years. Many governments are either implementing or considering restrictions by imposing limits on catches, curtailing the issuing of licences or other means. There is some hope that deep-water populations of conch may help to lead a recovery of this fishery if they are protected. Unfortunately even these animals now seem to be the target of short-term gain by some fishers.

The fishing of turtles is relatively unimportant commercially but there is widespread feeling among conservationists that these creatures should be accorded greater protection particularly at their breeding grounds. Whaling too is an unlikely topic for debate in the Caribbean although most would think of this activity as one confined to temperate or even cold waters. At present the only sanctioned whaling takes place from Bequia, a small island which is part of St Vincent and the Grenadines. A small operation there is still allowed to take two humpback whales per season under the Aboriginal whaling clause of the International Whaling Commission's (IWC) 1986 moratorium. However, since 1992, the

Caribbean members of the IWC have consistently voted in favour of repealing the moratorium. According to some sources this attitude has been encouraged and fostered by the strongly pro-whaling country of Japan which, it is claimed, pays the Caribbean countries' membership dues. Clearly, financial factors play an important part in this conservation debate and development economics need to be borne in mind by all the national players, both major and minor.

◆ Mangrove swamps

It has been noted on many occasions that mangrove swamps are regarded by many as wasted space unless 'developed', where development usually means draining and clearing the swamp for aquaculture, tourism, housing projects or industry. Such changes are often deleterious in the long term if not immediately. The swamp acts as a buffer protecting the inshore seawaters from land drainage, collecting both sediment and dissolved chemicals from runoff. This buffer action works the other way round too, with the mangrove zone protecting the land from the worst effects of wave action especially during storms and hurricanes. Add to this the absolutely vital role that mangrove swamps play as a highly productive and biodiverse nursery for a range of commercially important fisheries. Last but not least they have their own resident populations of plants and animals whose beauty and interest rival their utility. In the Caribbean it is probable that mangroves are underexploited in a sustainable way. Except for local fishers the swamps are mostly ignored or targeted for destruction. John Clark in his book on coastal zone management has listed 56 types of product that are gathered from mangroves worldwide. These include medicines from bark, leaves and fruit as well as the more obvious food and timber items. As ecotourism destinations probably only Trinidad with its famous Karoni Swamp has caught the public imagination. There are signs that the full value and potential of mangroves are beginning to be understood in the Caribbean but we must all strive to conserve the swamps that remain. Once destroyed, their regeneration is difficult and costly if not impossible.

◆ Seagrass beds

Much of what has been said about mangrove swamps can be said about seagrass beds. Because they are not above ground they are not candidates for development, but none the less they are often regarded by tourists and those providing for tourists as less preferable than a clear sandy seabed. However, like mangrove swamps, they protect both the shore behind them and, in the opposite direction, the sea beyond them. Again, like mangroves, seagrass beds 'export' food and nutrients to the nearby ocean as well as acting as nursery and feeding grounds to numerous species.

Seagrass beds are vulnerable to disturbance. They are often damaged by the anchors and propellers of boats, by dredging and sand mining and through coastal engineering work which may alter currents. Because of their accessibility they are often heavily fished, particularly using beach seine nets, resulting not only in diminished stocks but also in considerable damage to the grass beds.

With the deterioration of coral reefs many snorkellers and divers are coming to realize the wealth of marine life to be found in seagrass beds. Likewise local populations and agencies are beginning to appreciate the importance of these beds to the integrated marine environment around their coasts. That said, there is still much work to be done before these areas are given their full value and awarded the protection they deserve.

POLLUTION

This is not the place for an extended treatment of this huge subject. Also it is fair to say that although the Caribbean region suffers from the effects of a range of types of pollution, the situation is not so grave as in some parts of the world. Despite this relatively fortunate circumstance there is still much that can be done through the efforts of individual residents and visitors as well as by governments and non-governmental organizations (NGOs). The following points address some particularly obvious or important forms of pollution that are widespread in the region.

- **Solid waste** Sadly one of the most obvious forms of pollution in the region is that of discarded solid waste: paper, plastic, containers and packaging of all sorts litter many urban areas. Because many of these items float, they will wash up on to beaches should they find their way into the sea. Most are persistent and unless collected they will accumulate to the point of being a hazard to wildlife as well as an eyesore. Luckily many communities are beginning to realize the sordid nature of such garbage and projects have been initiated to encourage not only more sensitive initial disposal but also the collection of previously discarded debris. These efforts, often fostered by local groups as well as government, sometimes attract financial support from aid agencies. Sadly they concentrate their efforts close to centres of population so that the heaps of cans and plastic bottles that pile up in more remote areas such as mangrove swamps are rarely dealt with. However, the visually obvious nature of this problem means that it is likely to continue to attract attention until solutions are in place.

Fig 9.9 Modern solid waste is a particular problem. Much of it floats and persists in the environment. As a result it accumulates on beaches where it is unsightly and poses a range of hazards to people and wildlife. Some communities are becoming aware of these issues and waste collection and disposal programmes, often funded by NGOs, are being put in place.

Fig 9.10 Two male and a female magnificent frigate birds roosting in mangroves. Notice the garbage in the branches, including a plastic bottle on a line and some fine mesh netting. These are probably items that the birds have picked up during feeding and which of course pose a considerable threat to them. Entanglement in, or ingestion of, a range of types of garbage is a frequent cause of death in a number of seabirds and mammals.

- **Sewage** Many communities in the Caribbean do not have a piped sewage system. However, seaside developments that do have drains usually discharge their waste directly into the sea without any prior treatment. This is true even for many hotel and tourist facilities. The organic material discharged into the sea can have profound and detrimental effects on marine life, especially coral reefs. There are also the public health risks although to date the Caribbean bathers have not suffered to the extent seen in some parts of the Mediterranean Sea. The problems here are economic as it is extremely costly (and very disruptive) to install mains drainage and sewage treatment. There is also debate about the problems presented by the inorganic nutrients (nitrates and phosphates) in the effluents from treated sewage. These may promote eutrophication and many experts advocate primary sewage treatment only, whereby the bulk of the solids are removed but the remaining liquid is discharged without further treatment. Where the needs are greatest some work has been done but the smaller and more isolated communities may well have to wait for some time. In the meantime much can be done by considering the most suitable point for disposal into the sea. Some careful thought about relocating outfall pipes combined with a relatively small investment can have a considerable beneficial effect.

- **Sediments**   When forests are cleared or soil laid bare by agriculture, particles will wash away in rainwater. These sediments can find their way into the sea. In the past the material often was deposited in mangrove swamps where it simply became part of the swamp. With the reduction of such swamps and with the greater canalization of rivers, more sediment is being carried out into coastal regions where it can do great damage to reefs by depositing on the feeding tentacles of corals and other small animals. Not only is this a problem for the marine environment but also it reflects soil erosion on land, a process that can eventually lead to a great impoverishment of the local agriculture. Any move to reduce such erosion will benefit both land and sea. Education and guidance are helping here. However, mangrove swamp depletion still continues and more needs to be done to bring home an understanding of the role played by these swamps in protecting the reefs.

  Agricultural sediments will inevitably bring with them agricultural chemicals, fertilizers, herbicides and insecticides in particular. These also can have harmful effects on the inshore environment. In particular nitrogen and phosphate fertilizers can promote algal growth and eutrophication.

- **Oil**   Oil spills are thankfully infrequent and small in the Caribbean. When they do occur their effects can be devastating, especially to mangroves and the organisms that grow on the submerged roots of red mangroves. Pressure must be maintained on oil producers and carriers to ensure that the Caribbean never suffers an *Exxon Valdez* or an *Erika*. (This latter oil spill, resulting from the tanker running aground in northwestern France, did nearly US$1 billion worth of damage and killed more seabirds than any previous spill.)

INTEGRATION

Integration is the key word in dealing with the biology and conservation of the marine environment of the Caribbean. The major ecosystems that characterize the region, coral reefs, mangrove swamps and seagrass beds, all work together as an interdependent

Figs 9.11 and **9.12** These two pictures show the effect of an oil spill on mangrove roots: Fig 9.11 (left) shows a root unaffected by the oil with its rich fauna including many sponges and oysters; Fig 9.12 (below) shows roots from the same area that had been subjected to oil a few weeks previously. All of the fauna has gone except for the oysters and it is not at all clear whether or not they are still alive.

and integrated whole with complex movements of nutrients, organisms and food. Any impact on one part of the system will affect the others. Of course there are many places where one or two of these ecosystems operate in the absence of the others but only in the conjunction of all three is the full potential for Caribbean marine life developed.

The other side of the integration coin is the need for those people who impact that environment in some way to integrate their activities to minimize harm while maximizing opportunity for all. Human presence is inevitable. So long as the human race exists, mankind will wish to exploit the sea and coasts whether for pleasure or gain. Most Caribbean countries are small and relatively poor. In one way or another the sea provides many with the basis for a livelihood and any desire to protect wildlife must take these legitimate claims into account. The buzzwords are 'Integrated Coastal Zone Management' (ICZM). Such a management strategy has to reconcile numerous claims and to bring about a compromise that achieves the best aims of enlightened conservation as well as serving the needs of both citizens and visitors. There are many strands to this complex weave: legislation (and its enforcement!); environmental data; education; enlightened leadership at all levels of the community; inputs from interested parties; and (last but not least) money. There is no room in this pattern for cynical profiteering or short-termism. Sacrifices will have to be made but hopefully these will be spread widely as will the benefits.

Where conflicts of interests are few then it is possible for one major interest to dominate. For example in areas of great natural beauty where local populations are few and perhaps tourism is aimed at diving, it is possible to establish **protected areas** in which restrictions are placed on fishing, collecting and the use of anchors. A prime example of this is the small island of Bonaire where, since 1979, the waters around the island from the high water mark to the 200-foot (60 m) contour have been designated a marine park protected by law. In places with more than one major claim on the marine resource the creation of such protected areas, while seeming to be attractive, is politically more complicated. Furthermore, the declaration of a marine park may be fairly simple but policing and the enforcement of the legislation can be difficult (and often expensive). More and more it is being realized that it is particularly important to involve local people in the project. This is especially true if they are to lose access to earnings (through fishing for example) by the creation of a reserve. Often the solution may be to

Fig 9.13 Diving in protected areas such as marine parks is likely to be more rewarding than in exploited ones. Despite this general rule, good diving is to be found throughout the Caribbean.

involve them in the profits which accrue from the resultant increase in tourism. However, despite the problems, more and more such reserves are being created and they will undoubtedly play a major role in the conservation of Caribbean marine life.

Fig 9.14 A significant proportion of tourists is in the Caribbean specifically to dive. The environmental balance sheet for diving is a complex one with pros and cons. Divers and dive boats inevitably do some damage to the dive sites. On the other hand diving raises local awareness of the importance of conserving marine habitats. The creation of protected areas is also more likely to take place in areas of special interest to divers.

TOURISM

One of the major players in the complex web of marine resource usage is tourism. Its impact may be indirect through shoreside building and sewage disposal or more direct through tourist damage to reefs. In those parts of the Caribbean where diving is the major focus of tourism, fostering conservation is relatively easy but where the emphasis is on mass market 'sun, sea and sand' holidays the impact may be more negative. Of course the issue is enormously complex, particularly taking into account the economic importance of tourism to the region. Hopefully the interest in ecotourism, when conservation will be a prime consideration for the visitor, will increase. The Caribbean tourist industry should perhaps be doing more to educate their visitors (and, indeed, their operators) about the delights of the region's wildlife and the importance of its protection. For their part, tourists can do much by asking for more wildlife-based activities. There is no doubt that the increasing desire on the part of tourists to experience unspoiled environments as a specific part or major aim of their vacation has helped the receiving nations to focus on and justify conservation. Thus this type of ecotourism has helped to preserve habitats and encourage conservation. Furthermore, ecotourism can often help relatively poor local populations so that everyone benefits. As John Clark has written 'Integrated coastal zone management provides a mechanism to achieve a proper balance between use and preservation while increasing the likelihood of long-term survival of protected areas through resolution of potentially divisive conflicts that arise between competing uses of the coastal zone'.

CONCLUSION

As has already been indicated, there can be no doubt that enlightened conservation depends on reliable ecological data. Conservation after all is concerned with the maintenance of communities in their 'normal' state. Conservationists must know what is 'normal'; they must know what fluctuations are within the natural range and which are likely to be inevitable or deleterious. While perhaps it might be for the conservationists to define 'deleterious', it is for the ecologist to supply the hard data upon which such value judgements can be made. One particularly important project in the area of marine conservation in the Caribbean is the Caribbean Coastal Marine Productivity (CARICOMP). This involves some 27 marine laboratories around both the islands and the mainland coasts of the Caribbean. Most of these institutions send survey data to a processing and coordination centre in the University of the West Indies, Jamaica. The surveys, carried out using agreed standard methods, examine local undisturbed coral reefs, mangrove swamps and seagrass beds as well as taking measures of seawater and weather at the sites. Some institutions are not yet able to comply fully with the standards agreed but already there is a growing database of numerical information which will enable us to understand much more completely the changes which are taking place in these ecosystems and thereby to aid conservation policy and decision making.

As was said at the beginning of this chapter, ecological studies can be very simple. Specialists, like those contributing to CARICOMP, play a major role in ecological data collection but anyone can contribute to our knowledge of the environment. Indeed around the region the amateur and part-time ecologists have been very active both in their acquisition of useful data and in their valuable support of conservation. There are numerous examples of this type of contribution to the natural history and ecology of this area: Michael Humfrey's book on the shells of the Caribbean is the work of a Jamaican policeman; the *Flora of Barbados*, based in part on the flower collections of the Goodings; the publications, talks and display on Arawak and other archaeological remains by Desmond Nicholson in Antigua, highlight three very different areas of interest. Perhaps it is unfair to pick just three names as throughout the Caribbean the part-timers have been and still are an influential and formative influence in ecology, natural history and conservation.

What can be done to preserve the wonders and beauties of the Caribbean Sea? Those readers who have read through to this point will already be aware of some of the problems that have arisen as a result of Man's impact on the marine habitats. Clearly this drift towards the lowering of the quality of our environment must be stopped and if possible reversed. Suitable legislation can help to do this but much more important are the attitudes and desires of the population, both resident and visiting. In this respect education is of vital importance both in the formal institutions of learning and outside among the adults, not least among those who are influential in our societies. One of the most valuable things that this education can do is to encourage a simple love and appreciation of the animals and plants around us. Once that sense of joy has been experienced

Fig 9.15 Non-diving tourists also contribute positively and negatively to the state of the region's marine habitats. The key to increasing the former at the expense of the latter lies in better education of both tourists and residents. The rise of ecotourism is likely to have a generally beneficial effect on environmental understanding.

Fig 9.16 The vulture wheels! Hopefully not too fearful an omen for this north Jamaican seascape. The future lies in the hands of us all – old and young, rich and poor, resident and visitor. Each of us can make our contribution to a better Caribbean. (The bird, which is known as john crow in Jamaica, is more widely called the turkey vulture, *Cathartes aura*.)

the desire to preserve and protect that which is beautiful will follow automatically. This is one of the reasons why it is vital for teachers and educators to strive to get their pupils and students out into their environment as much as possible. Children may dirty their clothes and hands but their minds will certainly not be sullied. No amount of chalk and talk can substitute for that experience.

Conservation as a general policy is not founded on a conservative desire to deny change for no good reason, rather it is motivated by the need to preserve the goose that lays the golden eggs. Everyone in the Caribbean realizes that a proper supply of protein is essential to our well-being, and that various marine animals can contribute to that supply. The enlightened conservationist is interested not in reducing such exploitation but rather in maximizing it, *by having a regard to the long-term as well as the short-term consequences.* Conservationists must take pains to explain the logic of their advice for today's dollar speaks louder than tomorrow's in many minds.

Glossary

The terms are defined here in a way appropriate to this book. Some of them may have a wider meaning than the definition given here.

Abyss The deepest parts of the oceans and seas where there is no light and thus no growing plants.

Adaptations The ways in which an animal or plant is suited to its particular way of life.

Alga (pl. **algae**) A group of plants which includes all the seaweeds and the microscopic plants of the phytoplankton. The term can be used to apply to a particular seaweed (e.g. an alga).

Aquaculture The farming of aquatic animals. Mariculture is the farming of specifically marine (i.e. seawater) organisms.

Aquatic Living in or pertaining to water, either fresh or salt.

Bacteria Microscopic unicellular organisms. Each cell is much less complex than any cell of an animal or plant, in particular because they lack a discrete nucleus. Although some cause disease, many are involved in the breakdown of organic matter.

Barbel Tentacle-like growths from the lower jaw or mouth region of some fish. They are usually used as sensory organs for probing sand and mud.

Benthic Referring to the seabed and the organisms found there.

Brittlestars *See* Echinoderms.

Carnivore A meat-eating animal.

Chlorophyll A coloured pigment in green plants essential for photosynthesis.

Cilium *See* Flagellum.

Cleaners, **cleaning fish**, **cleaning shrimps** Fish and shrimps that remove ectoparasites from other animals (mainly fish). The cleaner organism is often brightly coloured and will advertise its presence to 'customers'.

Commensalism A relationship between two unrelated organisms where one gains a clear benefit while the other suffers no disadvantage. *See* also Mutualism, Parasitism and Symbiosis.

Community An ecological term for any naturally occurring collection of organisms living in the same environment.

Conch A group of snail-like molluscs. *See* page 82.

Conservation The protection, management and wise use of all living and non-living, cultural and human resources.

Coral A general term applied to many coelenterate animals that form a horny or limy skeleton. The hard corals are those which are mainly responsible for reef formation. *See* page 54.

Coral reef A submarine structure mainly made of the accumulated skeletons of hard corals usually covered with living coral. Some reefs are dead and have no living coral, while others may have been raised above the sea level to form coral rock. *See* page 52.

Crustaceans Members of the class Crustacea which is part of the phylum Arthropoda which also includes the insects. The crustaceans all have a jointed external skeleton and are mostly aquatic. The best known are the crabs and lobsters. *See* page 74.

Currents Movements of water created by either winds, tides or differences in salinity and/or temperature between water masses.

Cuticle A waxy layer secreted on to the surface of the leaf, one of whose functions is to reduce the evaporation from the leaf. *See* page 17.

Detritus Small fragments of material having their origin from living creatures, either by breakdown or excretion.

Echinoderms Members of the phylum Echinodermata. There are five main groups. *See* page 70.

Ecology The study of the relationship of living things in their environment. This includes both the interactions between the organisms and the interactions between them and their physical world.

Environment All the conditions or influences within a particular ecosystem which affect the organisms of that ecosystem.

Fauna All of the animals living in a particular place.

Filter feeding The process by which some animals filter out food particles from the surrounding water. They may do this by passively filtering moving water or by creating currents with their own movements.

Flagellum (pl. **flagella**) A tiny hair-like cell process used by microscopic animals and plants for locomotion. Many larger animals have surfaces, such as gills, covered by many similar structures. In such large groupings they are termed cilia (sing. cilium).

Flora All the plants living in a particular place.

Food chain and food web Seagrass is eaten by urchins which are eaten by fish. This is an example of a food chain. However, the situation is hardly ever so simple. Other things may eat the seagrass, urchins will eat other plants and fish will eat food other than urchins. A food web attempts to describe these complex feeding interactions.

Gastropods A group of molluscs that includes snails and slugs. Many are marine or shore-living.

Gills Filamentous structures used by marine animals for obtaining oxygen from the surrounding water. In some animals the gills may have other functions, e.g. food collection in filter feeding bivalves.

Habitat The specific, physical place where an organism or group of organisms live, e.g. in a hole, under a rock. In a broader way it can apply to an area with characteristic physical properties and a specific type of flora and fauna, e.g. a mangrove swamp or a seagrass bed.

Herbivore An animal that eats plants.

Igneous rocks Rocks which were once molten, e.g. rocks derived from volcanic lava.

Immature Not old enough to breed.

Invertebrates Animals without backbones including worms, crustacea, echinoderms and molluscs among many other groups.

Isopod A member of the crustacean group, the Isopoda. Some of these creatures are ectoparasites of fish.

Kilometre *See* Metric measures.

Larva (pl. **larvae**) The juvenile stage of many animals. The larva is usually different in appearance from the adult and may lead a very different way of life.

Luminescence The light produced by animals and plants. Many creatures have this capability, including planktonic organisms, worms and fishes. On land, the best known Caribbean example is the firefly.

Mammals Warm-blooded hairy vertebrates which develop their young in the womb and which then suckle their young after birth.

Mariculture *See* Aquaculture.

Marine Living in or pertaining to the sea.

Metre *See* Metric measures.

Metric measures This book uses imperial measures with metric conversions.

Some useful equivalents are:

1 centimetre is about 0.4 inch
30 centimetres are about 1 foot
1 metre is about 3.25 feet
1 kilometre is about 0.62 mile
1 kilogram is about 2.2 pounds
1 litre is about 1.76 pints
1 hectare is about 2.5 acres

Molluscs Members of the phylum Mollusca. There are three main sub-groups: the snails and slugs (gastropods) which creep on a flat foot and usually have a shell which is often spirally coiled; the bivalves, relatively sedentary creatures with a double shell within which the animal lives; the cephalopods which are active swimming predators including octopuses and squids.

Mucus A slimy secretion containing protein often used by filter and suspension feeders for trapping food particles.

Mussel A bivalve mollusc.

Mutualism A relationship between two organisms where both appear to benefit. *See* also Commensalism, Parasitism and Symbiosis.

Nudibranchs Shell-less molluscs related to the snails; sometimes called sea slugs.

Nutrients Substances which are necessary for healthy growth and development. Important nutrients for plants include nitrates and phosphates.

Oysters A group of bivalve molluscs members of which are often found growing on the roots of red mangrove trees.

Parasite and parasitism An animal or plant that lives on or inside another animal or plant to the host s detriment is a parasite. The mode of life is termed parasitism. Ectoparasites live on the surface of their hosts while endoparasites live inside them.

Pelagic Belonging to the deep oceans.

Pelvic and pectoral fins Most fish have two pairs of fins growing from their sides. The more forward and often slightly higher pair is the pectorals while the hinder and often lower pair is the pelvics.

Photosynthesis The manufacture of complex chemicals from carbon dioxide and water using light as the source of energy. This is usually a property of plants, the green pigment, chlorophyll, being essential in the process.

Plankton The animals (zooplankton) and plants (phytoplankton) which float in large bodies of water. The drifting plants constitute the phytoplankton while the animals make up the zooplankton. Planktonic creatures are most plentiful near the surface.

Polyp An individual of a colonial animal such as a coral.

Population Members of the same species living in a community.

Predator A carnivorous animal. Its victim is called the prey.

Prop-roots Roots growing out from stems, often tree trunks, at an angle which tends to support the plant. Red mangrove trees have many prop-roots.

Radula The file-like tongue of many gastropod molluscs, used for rasping their food.

Rectum The hindmost portion of the gut.

Salinity The saltiness of the sea. This varies from place to place. Ocean water (including that of the Caribbean) contains about 3.5 per cent salt while in the Red Sea evaporation of the water may raise this to 4.0 per cent. In the Baltic the salinity is much less than this due to the inflow of river water diluting the concentration.

Scavenger An animal that feeds on dead or dying organisms.

School A group of fish.

SCUBA Self-Contained Underwater Breathing Apparatus. This acronym is applied generally to the wide variety of equipment now available to permit free divers to descend to moderate depths carrying compressed air in cylinders. Typical amateur divers can stay under water from 30 minutes to an hour depending on the depth of their dive.

Sea anemones Animals belonging to the phylum Cnidaria which also includes the jellyfish. They are closely related to the corals.

Sea cucumbers *See* page 72.

Seagrass Marine plants that grow in shallow lagoons where they may cover large areas of seabed thus creating seagrass beds. They belong to the genera *Thalassia* and *Diplanthera*.

Sea-squirts Sedentary filter feeding animals with a larva like a tadpole. Thought to be related to the vertebrates.

Sea urchins *See* page 71.

Sedentary Applied to animals that cannot or do not move about much or at all, e.g. barnacles and sea anemones.

Sedimentary rocks Rocks originally formed as sediments on the beds of the seas, rivers or lakes, e.g. sandstones and limestones.

Spicules Tiny spines of hard material, usually calcium carbonate or silica, that support the tissues of an animal, e.g. sponges.

Sponges Members of the phylum Porifora. These simple animals, although containing many cells, are of very simple organization having no proper nervous system. They feed by sieving out food from the surrounding sea.

Starfish *See* page 70.

Substrate The solid surface to which animals are attached or over which they walk. Some substrates, e.g. sand, may be burrowed into.

Symbiosis An intimate and mutually beneficial relationship between organisms of different species, e.g. the coral polyps and their zooxanthellae. The participants in these relationships cannot usually exist independently of their partner. *See* also Commensalism, Mutualism and Parasitism.

Territory An area of the habitat usually occupied by a single animal of a particular species. The occupant will defend this territory against other members of its species. Territories may also be held by breeding pairs or by groups of the same species.

Tide The periodic (twice per day) rise and fall of sea level which is caused by the gravitational pull of the sun and moon. The size of these tides depends on the phases of the moon.

Toxic Poisonous.

Tunicates Sedentary filter feeding animals whose larvae superficially resemble a tadpole and have many features which link them to the vertebrates.

Turtle-grass A synonym for seagrass (see above).

Turtles Members of a group of mainly aquatic reptiles which also includes the tortoises and terrapins.

Vertebrates Animals with backbones including the fish, amphibia, reptiles, birds and mammals.

Zonation A term used in this book to denote the changes in fauna and flora in relation to differences in vertical height up or down a beach or submarine feature. Thus the plants and animals at the top or bottom of a beach will be characteristic of their position. Similarly the creatures on a coral reef slope will change in a characteristic way with water depth.

Zooxanthellae The symbiotic algae living in the cells of some animals, especially corals.

Bibliography

The following is not a list of sources, rather it is a list of identification guides to the animals and plants included in this book.

Alivizon, W. S. (1994) *Pisces Guide to Caribbean Reef Ecology*. Houghton Mifflin. ISBN 1559920777.

Clark, J. R. (1995) *Coastal Zone Management Handbook*. CRC, Lewis Publishers. ISBN 1566700922.

Humann, P. and Deloach, N. (1990) *Reef Creature Identification: Florida Caribbean Bahamas*. New World Publs. ISBN 1878348019.

Humann, P. and Deloach, N. (1993) *Reef Coral Identification: Florida Caribbean Bahamas*. New World Publs. ISBN 1878348035.

Humann, P. and Deloach, N. (1995) *Snorkeling Guide to Marine Life: Florida Caribbean Bahamas*. New World Publs. ISBN 1878348108.

Lee, A. S. and Dooley, R. E. (1998) *Coral Reefs of the Caribbean, the Bahamas and Florida*. Macmillan Education. ISBN 0333674022.

Nellis, D. W. (2001) *Common Coastal Birds of Florida and the Caribbean*. Pineapple Press. ISBN 156164191X.

Sutty, L. (1990) *Seashells of the Caribbean*. Macmillan Education. ISBN 0333521919.

Took, I. F. (1979) *Fishes of the Caribbean*. Macmillan Education. ISBN 0333269691.

The following four books are out of print at the time of writing but are worth looking out for in second-hand bookshops or libraries.

Chaplin C. C. G. and Scott P. (1972) *Fishwatcher's Guide*. Harrowood Books.

Humfrey M. (1975) *Sea Shells of the West Indies*. Collins.

Warmke G. L. and Abbott R. T. (1975) *Caribbean Seashells*. Dover Books.

Voss G. L. (1976) *Seashore Life of Florida and the Caribbean*. E. A. Seemann.

For general interest and very fine photographs the following is recommended.

Popov, N. and Popov, D. (2000) *Children of the Sea*. Macmillan Education. ISBN 0333735382.

Index